Loretta Fox holds a B.A. in English and an M.A. in Religious Studies. She has been employed by two Philadelphia-based hospice organizations and is also a trained hospice volunteer. Loretta has worked in several spiritual settings, most notably in the Archdiocese of Philadelphia (Catholic) and as Administrator of Abington Friends Meeting (Quaker). She has worked as a care manager for senior adults and as a teacher. She is also trained in Intuitive Spirit Communication, commonly called mediumship. She was raised in Philadelphia but currently lives in Maryland with her husband.

Visit LorettaFox.com for more information.

Dedicated to my mother, Ellen, of course
And to Scott, Abby and Zoe for holding me while I held her.

Loretta Fox

Walk Her Up the Stairs

A Caregiver's Healing
& Spiritual Journey

AUSTIN MACAULEY PUBLISHERS™
LONDON * CAMBRIDGE * NEW YORK * SHARJAH

Copyright © Loretta Fox 2024

The right of Loretta Fox to be identified as author of this work has been asserted by the author in accordance with sections 77 and 78 of the Copyright, Designs and Patents Act 1988.

All rights reserved. No part of this publication may be reproduced, stored in a retrieval system, or transmitted in any form or by any means, electronic, mechanical, photocopying, recording, or otherwise, without the prior permission of the publishers.

Any person who commits any unauthorised act in relation to this publication may be liable to criminal prosecution and civil claims for damages.

All of the events in this memoir are true to the best of the author's memory. The views expressed in this memoir are solely those of the author.

A CIP catalogue record for this title is available from the British Library.

ISBN 9781035821181 (Paperback)
ISBN 9781035821198 (ePub e-book)

www.austinmacauley.co.uk

First Published 2024
Austin Macauley Publishers Ltd®
1 Canada Square
Canary Wharf
London
E14 5AA

Table of Contents

Chapter 1: Getting There   9
   Preface to Prayer   *26*
Chapter 2: The Diagnosis   27
   To My Mother   *39*
Chapter 3: Unpacking It All   40
   Caregiver's Lament   *61*
Chapter 4: Becoming Routine   62
   Dusty   *74*
Chapter 5: Life with My Mother   75
   Breakdown   *97*
Chapter 6: The Beginning of the End   98
   My Mother's Thoughts (Maybe)   *114*
Chapter 7: Saying Goodbye   117
   Death Rattle   *134*
Chapter 8: Her Last Day   136
   Grief   *150*
Chapter 9: Life Without My Mother   153
   Throwing It All Away   *167*
Chapter 10: My Journey   169
   My Appetite   *184*

Epilogue: My Mother's Life and Legacy	**187**
My Mother's Life	*204*
Acknowledgments	**206**

Chapter 1
Getting There

"All this shibobble is so upsetting!"

My mother, Ellen, age 93

I didn't realize my mother was dying. She was still funny and feisty, and as annoying to me as ever. I would never have guessed that I was about to become her full-time caregiver.

When our final journey together began, all I had hoped to do was to convince her to move to a new home with us, and that was going to be enough of a challenge, given our history. If I had realized she was in her last months, things might have progressed differently. But then again, I think that the way opened, and all of the circumstances of our move lined up with all of the new information we were about to receive on her health.

In hindsight, it was probably best that I didn't see the whole metaphorical staircase before we had to take that first step, because I might not have started the climb. But when my husband was offered a new job out of state, I didn't yet envision the whole scenario, and I only wanted to convince my stubborn mother to move away with my family.

Aside from her early childhood in upstate Pennsylvania, my mother lived all of her life, quite proudly, within a ten mile radius of Northeast Philadelphia. So, I'm not sure why I thought that she, at age ninety-three, might agree to move. She was as much of a homebody as a person could be. Whenever someone from another part of Philly would ask where we lived, she would respond, 'We live in *Saint Williams*', as if the name of our Catholic parish identified the whole neighborhood, which it didn't.

Having been born in the mid-1920s, and having birthed me, the third of her three daughters, at age forty-one, her domestic bliss spanned the era of Suzy Homemaker and *Father Knows Best*, and both of those dated ideals were points of pride for her.

It didn't matter how much pain was hidden behind our Irish-lace curtains. Our rowhome on Alcott Street was meant to be our family castle. She put down her roots right through our tiny front lawn, and she and my father stayed as close as possible to that neighborhood until he died. Even when she was on her own as a widow, my mother wanted to remain in that familiar area and be near all the places we knew so well, including my father's grave in the cemetery where most of our relatives were buried. I knew that it would take some convincing to get her to move away, especially to live with me.

All of the issues were about to resurface for me in the coming months, but the foundation of our mother-daughter relationship had already been shaken a few times. I had already established myself as the disappointing daughter who left the Catholic Church. I had married a Jewish guy, and we had raised our daughters within a liberal Quaker community. In my family, that was pretty rebellious.

My husband and I even celebrated some Jewish holidays in addition to all the holidays I grew up with. I don't think my parents saw that coming. I had been a quiet and naïve kid, and all through my public school education, I was the goody-goody rule-follower with excellent grades in most subjects, except gym. I went through all twelve years of CCD classes for Catholic kids attending public school, and I eventually chose a Catholic college.

So, it was especially surprising to my parents that I was the daughter who eventually strayed from the Catholic path they'd chosen for their girls. I had developed my own free-thinking worldview, and I disagreed with most of my mother's opinions. My spiritual understanding was still evolving, but my mother felt that she knew the important answers, and her faith was her guidebook. I didn't really see much potential for us to ever reconcile our fundamental differences.

My husband's brother told me recently that he used to notice the tension in the room whenever our extended family got together for special occasions. He felt the strain mostly from me, but only when I was in the presence of my mother. To him, my mother seemed sweet and friendly, but he knew that she must have been upsetting me in ways he couldn't see, because my uneasiness was palpable.

My brother-in-law was right, of course. I was aware of the agitation coursing through my own body whenever my mother and I were together as adults, even if other family members saw her differently.

My mother was extraordinary in many ways. Mostly, those ways were good and wonderful and nurturing, but sometimes she could be extraordinary in her narrow-mindedness, her insensitivity and her need to control things. My mother and I knew exactly how to annoy each other with the maximum impact, and she was capable of hurting me almost to the same degree that she loved me.

At the point when I decided to speak with my mother about moving, I didn't know what was coming. Maybe it's true that ignorance is bliss, but I thought that my mother still had at least several years of life ahead, because she had been in excellent health for her age. She wasn't being treated for any health conditions, and at her check-ups every six months, her doctor often commented on her good health and great genes.

So, I didn't anticipate that within a few months I would become her 24/7 caregiver and be by her side when she died. Our time together was about to become more painful, but it would also lead to some healing. Our journey would transcend the ordinary world and open me to new and wondrous spiritual experiences, including learning mediumship—a skill that came as a surprise and continues to amaze me.

I didn't expect any of this as we were planning our move, but my mother's physical decline and her eventual mental decline would give me new insight into this remarkable woman's life and help me become more fulfilled. I simply couldn't foresee the complex and profound gifts that would come to me at the end of her life when our roles reversed and I became *the mother* to my mother.

I needed my mother to move with us because my husband, Scott, was taking a new job, and my mother couldn't be left in Philadelphia with no one nearby. Despite my exploration and travels in my early twenties, I was the daughter who settled close to my parents' home and provided most of the help they needed. I had become the person they could depend on for all of the practical things.

So, I thought that there was a chance that I could get my mother to agree to relocate with us. I suppose I did anticipate a battle, but I tried to stay as optimistic as possible.

"Mom, I have some good news to share with you!" I was holding my breath during this phone call, and praying for the right words, because I knew she'd be shocked. I deliberately didn't tell her in person, because face-to-face I'd lose my nerve and probably wouldn't say what I wanted. I pictured her sitting on her tidy beige loveseat in her fourth floor, climate-controlled apartment, holding her landline cordless telephone to her ear.

"You know that job I told you about, the one that Scott's being recruited for? Well, the recruiter says that they're going to make an offer to him in the next day or so."

"That's wonderful! He deserves something good like this," she replied, knowing that Scott had been in a miserable work situation for two years.

"Yeah, he really does deserve a good change. He loves this company, and if the salary is enough, I think he's going to take it." I paused to take a deep breath. "Do you remember that I said he could probably work from home, at least some of the time? Well, actually, they're going to want him on site. It's near Baltimore, so this means that we might have to move, if he gets an offer and takes it."

"Oh." She barely missed a beat before coming up with some negatives, as if she had already considered this possibility and had some responses ready. "You wouldn't want to live in Baltimore, though." She said it like it was a well-known fact. "The traffic is awful around there. Everyone says it. Traffic jams are all over the place in that area."

I tried to respond, saying that I wasn't really bothered by the hypothetical traffic. She asked if I was seriously considering this, and I said that I was. She exhaled loudly, showing her displeasure.

In case her point wasn't being made strongly enough, she went for the jugular. "And if you move, and leave your beautiful home here, what will you do if something happens to Scott? Then you'll be in Baltimore all alone!"

Wow. Did she really just say that?

She knew very well that Scott is almost fifteen years older than me. She probably figured that I worry about someday being alone, and she was right about that. I do worry all the time about outliving my husband, but I had enough sense not to talk to her about that. I'd known that she had not been happy about our age difference ever since our first date.

She made that clear at the beginning, along with her other objections about Scott, all of which turned out to be non-issues after we were married, because by then she often told him he was like a son to her. Still, during that phone conversation, I didn't expect her to jump to these killer negatives so quickly. In my gut, I knew that there was no way that she came up with those responses so fast. It was clear to me; she had thought about this possibility and rehearsed.

"Well, it will be hard, Mom," I said, fumbling, because the wind was knocked out of me.

I temporarily lost my ability to speak with confidence, but I kept on, just trying to get my message across. "We know all the cons, all the things that have to be considered, and we've been talking about it a lot. This isn't an easy decision at all, but Baltimore is less than three hours away from here, and this seems like it could be a really good move for us."

Just like her, I knew how to pause for dramatic effect, so I gave it a silent beat, while also trying to muster all my courage. Then I said, "Financially, we need this." She should have understood *that*. "With two girls in college, the tuition bills have been a struggle. You know that my job doesn't pay nearly enough to keep us here in Pennsylvania, and Scott would be so happy in this new job. It's a prestigious position for him in a think-tank on national healthcare. I want to support him in this."

She had the next argument ready immediately. "But won't you miss your beautiful azalea bushes? How could you leave them?" Well, I didn't expect the azalea argument. She really had thought this through.

"They have azalea bushes in Maryland, Mom, and this is something that would be really good for our family. If the offer comes through, I just want you to be prepared."

Then I said it out loud, although it was painful for me to even utter these words. "I want you to think about coming with us."

I heard her sucking in air, and even through the phone, I felt the giant 'No' floating in her breath. She didn't say it out loud though, and just stayed silent.

"I know that you love your apartment and being independent," I continued, "and I know that this would be a huge change, but there would be a few options if you came with us. You could get an apartment near our new house, or we could look for a house that's set up so that you could live with us."

No response.

"Or you could stay here, but then there'd be nobody close by to help you with shopping or emergencies."

Seriously, still no response?

"Mom, you know that you have to be near someone, right? To help you, I mean. I don't know how you'd manage if you were alone." Both of my sisters lived several states away. I'd been my mother's only helper for the past ten years, ever since my father died of lung cancer. "I want you to think about this, and we can talk about it, because we'll all have some decisions to make, and it seems like this is going to happen soon."

I desperately tried to stay positive and not let her know that this was hard for me too. The fact was that I was heartbroken myself, because I loved living in Glenside, Pennsylvania, where we raised our girls and where I'd felt at home for the past sixteen years.

Finally, she responded.

"I don't have to think about it," she said, resolutely. "I'm not moving."

Well, the next few days didn't get much better. In subsequent conversations, in person and on the phone, she repeated her arguments. She emphasized over and over that I could wind up *alone in Baltimore* if something happened to Scott, which made me want to cry every time she said it. She came up with more trivial things that would be missing if we left Pennsylvania, as if she was convincing me that I could never be happy in Maryland.

Looking back, I think that her words and attitude affected me more than I realized at the time, because I did struggle to feel at-home after we moved. Of course, we moved to Maryland in January of 2019, which gave me five months as her caregiver, followed by a summer and fall filled with grief. Then, I needed an unexpected minor surgery, which was immediately followed by a pandemic, and then two more surgeries on shoulder and foot injuries, as the pandemic continued.

These were not exactly the best conditions for settling in warmly and well, but we couldn't possibly foresee any of what was coming when we first had to make the decision about moving. My only goal was to figure out what Scott and I needed to do, and that meant that I needed to know what my mother wanted to do.

When Scott first told me about the prospective new job, he was excited and happy, and I could tell that it would be a life-changing experience for him to feel so worthwhile in a job once again. After a layoff two years earlier, he had done his best to find something solid, but the job he found at that time was not something he wanted. He had taken it because he was desperate. My salary as the administrator of a non-profit Quaker meetinghouse wouldn't cover our expenses, so he took the first offer.

He wound up with a commute that was over an hour each way, usually closer to two hours, and he came home at night exhausted and frustrated.

Then, when Scott was recruited for the new position, I could tell that he was energized by the idea of it. I was excited too, and I prayed that he'd get the offer. When it came through, with the condition that he relocates to the Baltimore area, I think I surprised him with my unconditional support. The truth was that I sort of liked the idea of a new adventure and the appeal of being anonymous in a new place.

I only knew one person in Baltimore, so I figured that I'd be able to go to the grocery store in sweat pants without make-up and not worry about running into any acquaintances, but beyond that over-simplification, I really did think it would be okay for all of us. We didn't have to worry about finding a good school district or children's activities. By that time, our daughters were grown, with one about to graduate from college in New York City that December, and the other in her sophomore year of college about an hour north of us in Pennsylvania.

Our girls were discovering their own paths, and each of them was bounding into adulthood free of the narrow views that I'd grown up with in my parents' house on Alcott Street. My older daughter, Abby, was about to start a communications career and was enjoying the non-judgmental feel of New York City. She was also becoming increasingly committed to her wonderful boyfriend, who happened to be a Mexican immigrant.

My mother loved him, partly because he had the same first name as my father, Alan, so she felt that my deceased father had a role in bringing them together. But I don't think she fully comprehended the immeasurable fears and struggles that immigrants constantly face. She seemed sympathetic to the fact that his family had more obstacles than most and that he had to work harder than many of his peers, and yet she routinely voted for candidates who were against meaningful immigration reform.

There was a sort of disconnect in my mother's thinking, because she knew that things were difficult for immigrants, but she didn't really perceive the overwhelming and disproportionate hardships. She seemed to think that because Abby's boyfriend was a good guy, bigotry would disappear and things would magically be okay for him.

My younger daughter, Zoe, was studying and exploring a career in musical theatre, and although she didn't officially come out to us as bisexual until she was in college, she was exploring her identity within the Queer community. She'd later tell us that she deliberately waited until my mother died before coming out to family and friends, and I completely understood that decision.

Yet, despite my mother's ultra-conservative Catholic perspective, my mother once told me confidentially that a beloved uncle of hers was, as she called him, 'a confirmed bachelor' and that she adored and appreciated him, although from what she told me, they never spoke about his sexual orientation. He never had a partner that she knew of, so it was okay with her that he was possibly homosexual, because he kept it quiet.

It was always clear that my mother never wanted to discuss anything too intimate, and she definitely held beliefs that were much less progressive than my own. So, I had not envisioned ever wanting to persuade her to move into my home.

However, when Scott got the job offer, it only took us about thirty seconds to register that this would also affect my mother. She had been living alone in the nearby apartment for just about ten years, and she had chosen the location because it was only a few minutes' drive from our house. She hadn't driven in years, but we could get to her quickly when needed, which was fairly often most of the time.

We drove her everywhere she needed to go—to doctor appointments, shopping, and errands—as well as to places that were just for pleasure. She spent a lot of time at our house too.

So, we thought about her, and we talked about her personality and her needs, and I told Scott that I couldn't imagine that she'd want to move to a new apartment. Even if it would be near our hypothetical new home in Maryland, she wouldn't want to feel so alone in a new place. However, he responded in a way that assured me that he absolutely wanted this job without question. He said that my mother should be invited to live with us in our home. He really, really wanted this job if he was willing to say that.

After the initial phone conversation with my mother, and the follow-up conversations, she stood firm. She was not going with us. I offered options, and she reluctantly considered them, because she realized that she simply could not continue to live independently without our nearby help.

I found information about daily housekeeping and nursing service, including grocery shopping and rides to appointments. I researched assisted living communities and narrowed the search to two that would surely be her favorites because they were Catholic facilities and quite lovely settings. We looked through full color brochures for each one, and I set aside time to talk with her about the cost.

I discussed all of this with each of my sisters, and both offered for my mother to come live with them. They invited her, and I encouraged her, although I knew from the start that she wouldn't go to live with either of them, because going to one of their homes would require an even longer-distance move.

I gently, but enthusiastically, proposed over and over that she could move with us, as Scott had said, right into our new home, wherever that might be. I told her that I'd show her everything I could find about houses in our target area, so that she could look them over too. She knew that the choice of a house would ultimately be ours, but she was being given veto power, as well as the opportunity to tell us what she'd envision as ideal.

When our conversations dragged on for days, and she continued to refuse to consider leaving the Philadelphia suburbs, I decided one day, after a particularly upsetting phone call, that I *was* going to take 'No' for an answer. We had been rehashing all the options, and she again fell back on listing all the negatives about the move, not only for herself, but for all of us.

She understood in theory that this was a marvelous opportunity for Scott, and she knew that it would be a benefit to our family financially, but she just couldn't get past her fear and worries. So, I said, "Okay."

I told her that she'd finally convinced me, and that I agreed with her that she should probably not move with us. In fact, I didn't want her to come any more.

The next day when I visited her, I again got out the brochures about assisted living places and the lists of in-home helpers, and I told her that she needed to choose something that would work for her. She needed to have a plan, because we had decided to move. I again explained that even if I had to leave my full-time job, Scott's new job had enough of an increase in salary that it would absorb the loss from my job.

So, I only had to find a part-time job in Maryland to have our family come out ahead. I told her that we were planning to move in December or January, and we were in October then, so it was coming quickly. I reminded her that my two daughters would be moving with us too.

Almost imperceptibly, I sensed the shift. I believe it's possible that up until I agreed with her that she shouldn't go with us, she thought that there was a chance that we'd change our minds and stay. When I suggested making concrete plans for her to stay behind, and reminded her that two of her beloved granddaughters would also be leaving the area, the reality hit her.

What she didn't know was that I wasn't bluffing. I really had changed my mind and felt at peace with finding her another situation for safe living. I felt some relief about not having her move in with us, because even while it was hypothetical, I knew how stressful it would be, how impossibly invasive it would feel to have her in my home twenty-four hours a day, with her knowing everything we did, every move we made. I was glad that we were going to find an option that did not involve taking her along.

But the pendulum swung pretty quickly, and she called me while I was at work the very next day to tell me that she'd made the *happy* decision to come live with us in Maryland!

Honestly, it felt like I'd entered *The Twilight Zone*, and I gritted my teeth and said that now *I* needed time to think about it. I reminded her of all the awful things she'd said to make me less sure of our future and less comfortable moving, and I told her that I had resigned myself to moving without her.

Really, though, I should have seen that coming. I should have known that she'd pick us over all the other options. She wouldn't want to be separated from us, and as she said, we knew her routine better than anyone. She was very close with my daughters, who shared the load of helping with errands and visiting her frequently. She often said that my girls were *her* girls.

They each had countless anecdotes of supermarket comedy with their grandmother, and stories about her passive aggressive ways to get them to take her to more places than planned, but they loved her as much as she adored them.

It took me only a few hours to call her back that evening and say that we were glad she decided to come along. I remember well that I tried again to enthusiastically describe all the things that we could do together, and how easy it would be when she didn't have to care for her own apartment and could relax. I listed the meals we'd make, and the fun we'd have being together around the dining table every single day. We talked about seeing horse farms in Maryland.

We discussed how things would be easier for me too, when she was under the same roof and I didn't have to worry about her being alone, and that was true. I knew that I'd miss having some physical distance between us, but it was resolved that she was going to come with us, and I was starting to accept that. We'd be together, and that was good for everyone, I thought.

I even told my mother that I loved the idea of my daughters being with their grandmother, reminding me of old episodes of *The Waltons* with everyone in the same house saying goodnight to each other at bedtime. That TV image really pleased her.

I only needed a day or so to catch my breath before talking with her about how we'd find a house.

Along with the job offer, Scott was given an allowance for moving expenses. "They're going to move us!" We said it as if it would happen with little effort, completely underestimating how much work was ahead. We'd moved before from Philadelphia when the kids were very little, but we'd been settled in Glenside, PA, for sixteen years, happily accumulating sixteen years' worth of stuff.

Scott's new company had a person on the team designated to coordinate our move, and we both spoke with her often enough to recognize her number when it popped up on caller ID. We were given the choice between two realtors to handle the sale of our much-loved Glenside home, and one realtor was assigned to work with us in Maryland. Her name was Cathy, and she also quickly became someone who knew us pretty well while trying to find us our ideal home in an area where none of the neighborhoods were familiar to us.

Meanwhile, we told our Glenside neighbors on Halloween that we were planning to move. When there was a lull among the children trick-or-treating on our street, Scott and I made the rounds to talk with our friends on the block to share our bittersweet news. We'd grown close with these folks, having block parties and dinners, and always taking time to stop and chat when we could.

Leaving those neighbors was incredibly difficult, and it felt appropriately Halloweenish and scary for me to be actually telling them that we were leaving. For me, that was the night that made all the moving plans seem concrete.

We had less than two months to find a house. Scott needed to be at his job in early December, so he was set to live in a residence-style hotel in the Baltimore suburbs until we could get there officially. We knew we couldn't move the whole house by December, but we were aiming for a move in January. We had a time limit for the company to cover the costs, and we didn't want to drag the process on longer than necessary.

In early November, Scott and I went to Maryland with Abby, who was home from college for a weekend. We spent the day with Cathy looking at paperwork and then visiting several houses. Nothing jumped out at us, although we tried to convince ourselves that there were two houses that we could make work. We knew we needed space for all of our own things, and also space for my mother and some of her things too. We went back to the homes without Cathy the following day to look again, but we were disappointed.

I planned a second visit to Maryland by myself about a week or so later, after scouring listings and compiling an impossibly long list of houses to visit. Cathy and I were both carrying large coffees when we met that Saturday morning, and we did a marathon of seeing twenty-two houses before we wrapped up well after dark that night. At the final house that day, Cathy and I were using our cell phone flashlights to find our way around an old three-story house with no electricity on.

Admittedly, there were quite a few of those twenty-two houses that were ruled out as we pulled up, so we didn't bother getting out of the car. Still, we went inside more than a few, and I started to get overwhelmed pretty quickly. Thankfully, I had the idea to record videos of the houses that seemed to be contenders, so that I'd remember which house was which later on when showing Scott. I was very disappointed, though, because every single house we visited that day had something that seemed to rule it out.

I drove home to Pennsylvania that evening, with a snowstorm imminent for the next morning, feeling dejected. I had been certain that I'd find 'our home' in that marathon day. Prior to the trip, I'd had a dream in which my dad told me that he'd help me find the house. Really. I'm not making that up.

In the ten years since my father had died, I'd had quite a few experiences of feeling his presence around me and knowing that he was urging me in the right direction. It was because I sensed him shortly after he died pushing me to convince my mother to move out of their house in Philadelphia, where she struggled to manage the daily tasks by herself, that I spoke to her about looking at apartments.

She and I had that conversation on St. Patrick's Day just a month after he died, with both of us feeling my Irish father's influence, and she agreed on that very day to start the search for an apartment closer to my family's home.

This sense of a spirit presence wasn't anything new to me, as I'd always been fascinated by spiritual things. It started as a desire to deeply understand the Catholic religion I'd grown up with. When I was a teenager, I actually visited a convent with a friend of mine with an earnest interest in possibly becoming a nun. My mother couldn't have been happier.

The convent was in the back of a Catholic bookstore in downtown Philadelphia. My friend and I ate a modest lunch (which we later suspected was the nuns' own lunch, since they didn't eat with us), and the nuns told us about their work in the bookstore. They showed us videos of themselves enjoying ridiculous outdoor sports, such as a softball game in which they were using a giant red plastic toy bat, while dressed in their full nuns' habits with veils flying in the wind.

I'm sure we were supposed to be impressed by their work and recreation, but we found ourselves giggling instead. This order of nuns was called The Daughters of Saint Paul, and as we left their bookstore that day, my friend and I quickly nicknamed them *Saint Pauli Girls*, like the beer, so it was fairly clear that we weren't appropriate for their mission.

As an undergraduate in a Catholic college, I majored in English to study creative writing, poetry and literature, but I also did a minor in Theology. Within that minor, I studied Catholicism but also focused on classes featuring other world religions. Later, I received a master's degree is in Religious Studies from a Catholic seminary, and it seems that with all that background and interest in Catholic studies, I would have wound up being deeply rooted in the Catholic faith (which in some ways, I still am).

The problem was that the more I learned, the more I questioned. That constant questioning was the beginning of my true spiritual journey, one that would be a long, twisting road, and one that would leave my parents' hopes for me in the past.

It began, perhaps, when I spent a year in the Jesuit Volunteer Corps when I was age twenty-three, a year after my graduation from college. I took a break from my master's degree studies to go to rural Washington State as a volunteer, living and working on the Colville Reservation. That year was life-changing, as my five roommates and I lived in a broken-down trailer home, with all the energy and eagerness of young adults, while working with the Native American community there.

I had the opportunity to witness and learn about the spirituality of the indigenous people in that area, including Coyote stories, sweat lodges, drumming, and respect for the Great Spirit. My eyes were opened to vast possibilities.

Years later, still interested in varying world-views, I found myself studying Shamanism, through an intensive small class with a woman who had been trained by shamans in Guatemala and had become a shaman herself. Together, we explored Shamanic Journeying to the Lower World and the Upper World, finding Power Animals and Spirit Guides.

Around that same time, I also found a teacher and learned Qigong, a Chinese moving meditation, and other Eastern practices for strengthening and healing of mind, body and spirit.

Throughout my life, I'd felt a pull toward Quakerism, where I eventually found my community. I loved that this was a religious practice that encouraged exploring questions, rather than assuming we have all the answers.

I also began learning about Spirit Mediumship, which spoke to my heart, but I had yet to realize that it would be something that I'd eventually be able to practice myself. Really though, I'd known all my life that spirits are around us, even when we don't experience them with our earthly senses of sight, hearing and touch. We sense them in different ways. I felt it on the day that Cathy-the-realtor and I were looking at the twenty-two houses near Baltimore.

There was one house. One house in that overwhelming day. One that felt like it had real possibilities and Cathy said it as soon as we pulled into the driveway. She liked it better than all the others we had seen. The outside was neat and tidy, but it didn't thrill me. Still, I knew that the exterior could be fixed up to my liking just by replanting the garden and adding some minor features. I went inside thinking that maybe I'd find a sign that reminded me of my father.

The inside was spacious, with plenty of room for my family of four plus my mother, and it was actually a bit larger than our Glenside home. It also had a back deck with a spectacular view into the woods behind the neighborhood. There were a few things I didn't love, such as the very awkward and ugly (in my opinion) large shelf in the living room, which extended out about a foot, and ran the whole length of the wall, almost into the dining room. It was brown faux marble with metallic gold trim on the front edge. It reminded me of a brown faux marble coffee table that my mother-in-law had years earlier. The shelf was about the height of a chair rail, but there was no way that a chair could be placed against that wall, because the shelf stuck out too far.

I also really disliked the giant Lucite chandelier, and I had difficulty envisioning the living room and dining room without those features. I realized that my mother-in-law would have liked that chandelier too, but our styles were very different. While I walked through the house, memories of her swirled through my mind, because this house would have suited her taste. So, I didn't necessarily feel my father there, but I, surprisingly, felt my mother-in-law.

Still, I knew that my dad would have liked the crisp cleanliness of the whole house, and the fact that it seemed to be in good repair. The house really was impeccable and the current owners had even required that we cover our shoes with paper booties, which were in a box by the front door, just to walk through. We found fresh carpet and paint throughout, with a full finished basement that would make a great family room and four bedrooms upstairs.

The house also had a den with a powder room nearby, and I could imagine my mother spending happy afternoons in that den, with plenty of room for her own living room furniture and feeling like she still had her own space within ours. This house could work for us, but it had its own deal-breaker which was the cost. It was way out of our price range, so although I recorded my videos of the interior and exterior, I let it go from my mind as we drove away.

After I drove back to Glenside that night trying to beat the snowstorm, I sat on the sofa with Scott and we looked through all my videos. I'd told him that I was disappointed, and I think I even told him about the dream I'd had beforehand with my father saying that I'd find a house that day. I'd thought I would come home with good news. Instead, I was glum, but I showed Scott my findings anyway.

When we came to the videos of the house with the shelf, as I'd nicknamed it, Scott asked me what was wrong with that one. He watched the videos from that house carefully, and he said that he didn't see any significant problems that couldn't be easily fixed. The shelf could be removed and the chandelier could be changed, and he thought the house was otherwise perfect. Then, he saw the price.

But he also saw something that I hadn't noticed. This house had been on the market for six months already, and the price had been dropped twice before. Well, that was interesting.

We called Cathy the next morning and discussed it with her. She advised us to offer the high end of our price range, which was still far lower than the asking price, and see what the owners would say. So, that's what we did. As expected, they came back to us with a firm 'No', but they asked if we could go any higher. At that point, we didn't feel that we could.

As I had promised, I showed my mother the videos from the houses I'd explored. There was one other house that had potential because it had an actual apartment on the basement level, and it was fully functional and quite nice, but I knew that my mother wouldn't like sleeping downstairs. She always said that she didn't want to sleep on the first floor because that's the place *bad-guys* would get to first when they broke in during the night.

So, she nixed that one quickly, as I'd expected. When I showed her the videos from the house with the shelf, she agreed with Scott that it seemed perfect for us. I told her that we'd made an offer but that it was too low to be accepted, and that we'd keep looking.

But as always, my mother had her own goal fueled by determination, and she liked that house. She liked that she could furnish the den as her own living space on the main floor, and she loved that her bedroom would be upstairs among the family bedrooms where she'd feel like part of the household, not separate. Without hesitation, she offered us a few thousand dollars from the money that she said she'd have to pay anyway if she went to assisted living, and she instructed me to call the realtor and try again.

I tried to argue about taking her money but she insisted, saying that she wanted that house. She said that she knew my father would have wanted her to give us some money so that she could live in that specific house with us.

There he was. He was guiding her as well as me. I felt my dad with me so much during those few days. It was like he was standing right behind me, gently nudging me forward with every step.

So, I was delighted and thrilled, but not really surprised, when the owners accepted our slightly higher offer at the end of that week with the only stipulation being that we make settlement before the end of the year, which was just a few weeks away. Actually, that worked out perfectly for us, because we also wanted to move as soon as possible so that Scott didn't have to be in the hotel for too long. We had hoped to get settled into our new home in the beginning of the new year.

Our home inspection went beautifully, and again I was relieved but not really surprised, because my father would have loved a successful home inspection, and I felt him with me that day too. The inspector actually told us that ours was one of the best home inspections he'd ever done. Our new house was in good shape.

We moved from Glenside, Pennsylvania to Owings Mills, Maryland in January 2019, into our beautiful new home, where I most definitely felt the presence of both my father and my mother-in-law. I felt well-protected and I felt much love, in this new place.

My mother moved a week later when I went to get her from her apartment in Pennsylvania. My eldest sister had come to stay with her and help her pack, giving us a few days to unpack some boxes in Maryland before my mother joined us. It also gave us time to set up a bedroom so that she'd have a comfortable place to sleep on her first night with us.

That was especially important, to make her comfortable right away, because my mother had received a terminal diagnosis just two weeks before we moved. Two weeks when everything changed. Two weeks that pulled our focus from our imminent move to my mother's imminent decline. Two weeks for me to process that I was going to have to become her caregiver, in a place where nothing would be familiar. I suddenly knew that my mother was going to die, and likely in our new home.

Preface to Prayer

God used to be my bicycle
ten speeds for every emotion,
and once there was an entity other than me
the great poet master general
who beamed light into my pen
without even a simple Shazam!
My Captain Marvel caped saviour
like the radio God on WMGK singing magic signs.
God went on my walks
narrated my novels
until I stopped needing and started reading
comic books. Now I only want
to know what's already written
in the speech bubbles
above my head.

Chapter 2
The Diagnosis

"When airplanes fly by way up in the sky, I wonder what they think when they look down and see the beautiful tablecloth on our deck table. I'll bet they love it!"

My mother, Ellen, age 93

"She's appropriate for hospice," her primary doctor of many years said without hesitation when I asked the question at her follow-up appointment.

In early December, my mother had started feeling short of breath and dizzy. She fell twice in her apartment, and both times she said that she felt herself about to topple over. The first time, she fell forward into her hall closet and crawled back out to pull herself up leaning on a chair. The second fall happened in her dinette area, and she would have hit the floor if the table hadn't caught her.

She said she was more embarrassed than hurt. She thought that both falls were hilarious, and she laughed hard each time she told me about falling. She definitely downplayed the severity and tried to make each one seem like a silly accident, but it seemed clear that something was going on with her. These falls were unusual.

We all felt certain that it was the stress of having to move.

I felt guilty. I had pressured her into moving with us, even though I knew it would be hard for her. Yes, we had to do what was best for my family, but I recognized that this was a terrible strain for my mother, especially because I knew her personality so well. She would sit and worry all day, second-guessing all decisions, and struggling to make sense of such a significant change in her lifestyle.

On one hand, she had come to fully accept that she was going to live with us, and I believe that she actually felt happy about the idea of being in our home together, but on the other hand, she was pulling up her roots and doing something that she had initially been strongly opposed to. I knew that. I tried to ease her worries. Yet, I tried, sometimes with clenched teeth and a forced smile, to stay positive in spite of all her expressed concerns, but I knew that the stress of moving was possibly too much for her to carry.

In hindsight, however, this could not have worked out any better than it did. Our upcoming move was exactly what she needed, because the new house would allow her to stay at home through her illness, which couldn't have happened in her present living situation. We were on the right track but I just didn't realize it at the time.

In mid-December, I took her to a routine doctor appointment for her six month check-up, and she told him about her recent symptoms, including the falls and also some tightness in her chest. We had told him that we both thought it could be stress and anxiety, but as he held his stethoscope to her chest during that initial visit, the look on his face told me that he suspected it could be more than stress. He found that her feet and legs were swollen, something that I hadn't seen because she was always in long pants when I visited.

His nurse did an EKG right there in the office, which showed some changes in my mother's heart, and the doctor said the changes seemed minor. But he heard a heart murmur, so he ordered more tests and prescribed a water pill for her.

As we left the office, her doctor pulled me aside while my mother was paying her co-pay and happily chatting with the receptionist. He told me that he suspected 'some heart failure' which would be normal for her age. He said that the treatment would be the water pill anyway, so the tests he ordered would just help to make a complete diagnosis. He told me that he wouldn't advise anything intrusive for treatment, and I completely agreed.

I asked him to follow up with me as soon as he had test results, since she had given me full access and permission to speak to her doctors, as well as power of attorney, years before.

But I didn't keep secrets from her, so shortly after we left his office, which was in the hospital's medical building, I told her what he'd said. I wasn't sure if she fully understood, but she really didn't have to. I was sort of glad that she wasn't getting more upset. She seemed relieved that the appointment was over.

I took her for bloodwork that same afternoon, since we were already at the hospital, and I remember the long wait at the hospital lab. There was a small Christmas tree in the corner, and carols were playing on the piped in music. I knew that she was nervous because she reached over to take my hand a few times, and we sat there talking about holiday plans, hand in hand.

When her bloodwork was done, we scheduled her echocardiogram a few days later, and I brought her to my house for dinner that night. My younger daughter, Zoe, picked up take-out food, so we had a relaxed evening with Zoe and Scott, talking and laughing, even though I was a bit on edge.

About a week later, Scott and I drove to New York City to pick up Abby at the conclusion of her final semester of college, since she was graduating a semester early. We had done the mad search for a parking space on the crowded Manhattan street, and she and Scott lugged her suitcases and bundles into the back of my minivan, making a few trips up to her room in the high-rise's elevator while I stayed by the car.

It was an emotional day, but Abby was so happy and relieved to be done with school, even though she didn't know exactly what the next step would be at that point. We were enjoying the drive home on the New Jersey Turnpike, talking about job possibilities for her, when my phone rang. The caller ID told me it was my mother's doctor. I answered on speaker phone, and I asked Abby to take notes of anything important that was said, because I was driving at that point.

It was actually the scheduler from the doctor's office calling, and she told me that the doctor wanted my mother to come back for a follow-up appointment.

Oh, no. That can't be good. If he wanted us to come back, something was really wrong.

I knew my mother well enough to know that she wouldn't want to be bothered with medical appointments during the holidays, so I scheduled it for January 3. When I talked with her about it, she agreed and adamantly insisted that she didn't want to see the doctor before January. She wanted to enjoy the holidays.

Yet, that was the first time in years that my mother wasn't with us at my house for Christmas. By the end of December, she wasn't feeling well at all, and she still had bruises from the falls. She complained more and more about the tightness in her chest, and she said that sometimes she had trouble catching her breath. Even though my eldest sister and her family were visiting us for the holidays, my mother didn't feel well enough to come to my house, so we took Christmas dinner to her apartment and visited her in shifts on Christmas and throughout the holidays.

On Christmas Eve, my daughters and I, as well as Abby's boyfriend, Alan, went Christmas caroling at my mother's door, and she loved that! Alan was a good sport and even rang jingle bells while we sang *We Wish You a Merry Christmas* as my mother stood in the doorway with her cane, laughing.

We had a graduation party for Abby on New Year's Eve, with a bunch of her friends as well as family friends, also making it a final blow-out party in our Glenside home, but my mother didn't come to that either. My middle sister came for a post-holiday visit just before we moved, and my mother stayed at her own apartment then too, with us going there and bringing carry-out food for meals. My sister spent some time with her while I continued to pack my house.

When January 3 finally rolled around, my mother and I sat in the doctor's office at the follow-up appointment, she with her list of questions and me with my own. The doctor confirmed that the tests showed that she had Congestive Heart Failure, which was a severe heart disease in her case, and that this would be something from which she would not recover. The change in her heart was fairly sudden, as she had been examined just six months earlier and nothing was detected then.

This time, the diagnosis was clear. She had a second or third degree blockage in her heart which meant that a pacemaker was needed. However, in her overall condition at age ninety-three, she wouldn't withstand the surgery, so he was recommending palliative care.

He told us that a heart blockage like my mother's is the type of thing that can cause a more quiet and quick decline, rather than lingering at the end. There was no real prognosis timeline. She could still have many months, but the unfinished thought hung in the air as he said that—many months *until she died*.

So, I asked the question about hospice and he said that her diagnosis was appropriate for hospice care, but I didn't just spring that question in front of her. I had prepared her ahead of time. In fact, after the phone call asking us to come back for a follow up appointment, I anticipated the hospice possibility. I wanted to protect her from the shock of hearing that word first in his office, so I brought it up before we went to see him.

I went to her place a couple of hours early to pick her up for the appointment, and we had the conversation then. We were sitting in her living room, in her too-warm apartment, with her seated in my father's old green recliner, which had become her special chair in the years since he passed, and me sitting on the bench next to her so that she could see my cell phone. I wanted to show her some website photos because I had already begun to do some research. This was as urgent as it was sensitive.

I needed to use my power of persuasion, and I knew that my mother trusted me. Even when I was a little girl, I seemed to be able to talk her into doing things. My sisters, being six and eight years older than me, were often doing more grown-up things than I was, and I spent a lot of time playing alone or doing things with my mother. My mother was a month shy of forty-one years old when I was born, so she was a little older than the mothers of many of my friends, but that didn't stop her from being my playmate, when she wasn't doing housework.

Still, my mother couldn't possibly have wanted to spend all those countless hours in my bedroom listening to my record collection on my portable record player, but we did it, night after night, after dinner and before bed. She did it because I wanted her to. She wanted to spend time with me. She'd sit on the edge of my bed for hours while I knelt behind her and brushed her hair, giving her exquisite 1970s hair-dos, explaining to her the meaning behind each song, probably making it sound as if I was a renowned music expert at age ten, while she was a complete moron.

But she never complained and always made me feel as if she loved it, loved being with me. I know now that this woman who adored classical music, opera singers and big bands was obviously only listening to Shaun Cassidy, Andy Gibb and Queen just to please me. Although, I suspect that she really did learn to love The Beatles and parts of *Bohemian Rhapsody*. But that's not the point. The point, which I have since come to treasure, is that even when I was a kid, she listened to me.

I tried to channel that same kindred spirit vibe when I prepared her for the hospice conversation. I had worked as a Coordinator of Volunteers for two local Pennsylvania hospices when I was in my late twenties, so I was very familiar with the hospice philosophy and mission. Unlike many people who think that hospice should only be called in at the very last minute, I understood that involving a hospice team early on in a terminal diagnosis can be a wonderful approach to care.

The motto I'd learned during my years working in hospice was that while we can't add days to one's life, we can try to add life to one's days.

I fully expected that my mother was going to need that kind of care, and I actually thought that it might be a relief to have a hospice referral in place when we moved. The hospice team, as I knew, consisted of a primary nurse, a social worker, a chaplain, a home health aide, if needed, and volunteers to serve as friendly visitors when requested. Additionally, the hospice patients are under the care of a medical director, and that meant that my mother wouldn't have to find a new primary physician in Maryland.

She had been really worried about finding a doctor that she would like as much as the one in Pennsylvania, because she had been with that practice since long before I was born. Even my grandparents had gone to that practice, back when it consisted of one doctor with an office in the front of his Philadelphia rowhouse. Over the years, the practice expanded adding more doctors, while some doctors left or retired, but my family stuck with them, mostly because my mother loved our long history with that practice.

She felt that all of the newer doctors were extensions of that original doctor. Scott used those same doctors too, as we found out when we started dating, and he and I continued to go to them. So, as we planned to move, Scott and I and our daughters were going to have to find new doctors, but my mother would be all set if she went onto hospice care.

When I started to suspect the direction we were headed with my mother's health, I had the idea to quickly research some hospices in Maryland. Actually, the idea to look up hospices came to me like a lightning bolt on the morning of her follow-up appointment, while I was in the waiting room of the dentist, waiting for Zoe to have her teeth cleaned one last time before we moved, because we were going to have to find a new dentist after we moved too.

It seemed like I was cramming all the appointments into the few days we had left in Pennsylvania. I had been sitting there in the waiting room lost in my sad thoughts, thinking about my mother's appointment coming up that afternoon, and imagining that we might possibly hear the news that she's nearing the end of her life. I thought about my father and all that had happened when he died, and then as I was thinking of him, the idea just hit me.

If she's possibly going to need hospice care, then I should talk to her about that and be prepared before we see the doctor.

I suddenly realized that I'd have to know what's available in Maryland before we move.

I'd be heading to my mother's apartment in just a few hours. So, right there in the dentist's waiting room, I started to search on my phone for hospices near our soon-to-be zip code. The first one that popped up had a name that was like an answer to a prayer. Stella Maris.

Given my background and studies, I knew instantly that the name was a reference to Mary, the mother of Jesus. Clearly, Stella Maris was going to turn out to be a Catholic-run hospice. As I scrolled through, I saw that it was under the care of the Sisters of Mercy, and I may have actually started to smile at my phone while sitting there in that blue vinyl waiting room chair.

One of my mother's closest friends was a Sister of Mercy, so this was going to be perfect. Even though I had left the Catholic Church many years prior, I knew that this was going to be of primary importance to my mother. She would trust this Organization. She would feel well cared for if her hospice team was sent by Stella Maris, and honestly, I think I shared the belief that the Sisters of Mercy would have trustworthy caregivers.

I found one other hospice listing for our local area in Maryland, but I barely noted them, because I absolutely knew which one my mother would prefer. When we got home from the dentist, I bookmarked the Stella Maris website and took notes about their history and mission. When I arrived at my mother's apartment a little later, I was completely prepared and ready to say the word *hospice* without fear of upsetting her. I decided to lead with the Catholic name.

"Stella Maris Hospice is near our house in Maryland," I told her, knowing that she had probably prepared herself to hear whatever the doctor might say today with her customary gracefulness of spirit, always making the best of things in any situation.

"It's run by the Sisters of Mercy," I continued, "and it's a hospice program that cares for patients in their own homes. It's for patients who have serious illnesses and aren't going to recover. Depending on what the doctor says today, we might want to think about something like this for you. The patients usually have a caregiver, like me, in their home, and then the professionals come and go as needed."

"This might be a good option for you, and you wouldn't have to find a new doctor in Maryland, because they have a medical director who would oversee your care."

It didn't take as much persuasion as I'd thought. She agreed quickly and wholeheartedly.

In fact, she seemed excited about it.

"Oh! The Sisters of Mercy! I'd love to have nurses from there!"

"Mom, the nurses won't be Sisters. The Sisters are probably in some of the offices, but the nurses and staff won't necessarily be nuns." I wanted to make that point clear to avoid problems down the road, when she might assume that every person who would come to care for her would be a nun.

"I know that!" she countered. "But if the Sisters are involved, then this will be a wonderful program. It's so lucky that you found them! I really hope that the doctor puts me on hospice. Let's ask him about that today."

Okay, I guess that's what I was hoping for, but I was suddenly worried that maybe she didn't fully understand the hospice meaning. I had the urge to remind her that it involves a terminal diagnosis, usually estimating six months to live. But I wasn't going to go there, because I'd much rather have her feeling secure about all that might be ahead.

Wasn't it better to have her being somewhat misguided than feeling the full effect of the diagnosis and prognosis? I wasn't sure.

Throughout her life, my mother had been a person who tried to make the best of everything. That was a real gift when it was a lemons-to-lemonade situation, because she laughed easily and often, and she was especially useful when anyone needed to be cheered up. But sometimes she tried to make the best of things when even when it wasn't appropriate.

I remembered too well being in the oncologist's exam room along with my parents when my father had been told that his lung cancer was inoperable. It was a shock and I barely knew what to say. As I drove us back to their house afterwards, we made strained small talk during the car ride, but then when we got into the house, my mother immediately said that she wanted to call my sisters to update them right away.

I sat there with my mouth gaping as I heard her tell both of them the same thing, "We just had Daddy's appointment, and the oncologist said that they don't have to operate!"

Obviously, I called both of my sisters later when I got home to my own house, and I explained exactly what the doctor had said, but it was a perfect example of the spin my mother could so easily put onto reality, especially when she wanted things to be different than they were. She did that often with things that affected my father.

Once, a few years after he had died, she and I were at the supermarket with my daughter, Abby, and we ran into the daughter of one of my dad's friends. The woman, who was about my age, seemed delighted to see us, and after hugs all around, she told us that she often thought about my dad with such respect and gratitude for all the help that he had given to her father through the AA program.

She and I both remembered our dads tending bar together at the Knights of Columbus Hall, because sometimes we were allowed to come along and play together at one of the tables off to the side, or if we were really lucky, behind the bar! We remembered the carefree times at that bar, and although we didn't say it out loud, I knew that we both also had memories of the frightening times when our dads would come home with red bloodshot eyes, smelling of alcohol.

It didn't take much to bring all those memories rushing to the surface for me. All the times my dad stumbled in the door, yelling and demanding. All the times he hollered at my mother, at my sisters, at me. The times when he was completely unreasonable. The times when he hit us, and the times when he tearfully apologized, bringing pizzas or snacks home to show that all was well again.

The painful memories flooded back, but I also remembered that it eventually stopped. He became himself again in the long run. Not perfect, but wonderfully my dad. And I stopped being afraid of him.

As we stood there in the aisle of the supermarket, this woman told us that before her own father passed away, he spoke so highly of my dad and the support he appreciated so much. She emotionally remembered that our fathers really helped each other through the process of recovery.

But when we got back into my minivan with our shopping bags ready to head home, my mother was outraged. She angrily whispered to me across the front seats, whispering in an effort to keep Abby from hearing, although I knew Abby could hear every word. My mother said that she could not understand how this woman could stand there and tell such lies about my father.

"He was *never* in Alcoholics Anonymous," my mother said, as if AA was something to be ashamed of. "He got a little bit tipsy once in a while when he was out with friends, but he was never a drunk." She spoke with complete distain.

"Now, *her* father, *he* had a problem. And Daddy helped him. But Daddy was nothing like *him*. I don't know how she could stand there and talk about them as if they were alike." I glanced in the rear-view mirror to see Abby reacting with raised eyebrows and then a grimace. Abby had already heard some of my stories from my own childhood and she knew better.

I couldn't help feeling that my mother was taking something away from my dad with that attitude. If she denied that he had a drinking problem, then she also took away the triumph of his recovery from it.

I remembered all the times growing up when my mother would rush around the house closing all the windows when our family had raised-voice arguments. She didn't want the neighbors to hear or know, although my friends who lived on our street assured me, by their curiosity and questions, that they did hear. Apparently, my dad's angry voice could penetrate glass. But my mother was an expert at covering up negative things, and also at rewriting history to make things seem better.

I suspect now that she needed that skill for her own sanity and survival.

Still, the making light of everything tactic didn't always work for her, even in later years.

When she lived in her apartment after my dad had died, her next door neighbor became a good friend, and since that woman was still driving, she and my mother often went out to lunch and did errands together. But one day, as they were returning home after an adventure, her neighbor's key got stuck in the doorknob lock. She couldn't turn the key, and couldn't get into her apartment.

The woman got upset, telling my mother that this had happened twice before and that the maintenance team didn't fix it correctly. She was annoyed and wanted to get into her place, but she had to use my mom's phone to call down to the management office to ask them to send someone. Apparently, while my mom and her neighbor were standing in the hallway as the maintenance guy worked on the lock, my mother started to laugh about the situation and said that it could have been worse.

"At least you were able to get into my apartment to use the phone," she said, "and thank goodness it's not late at night." Then my mother added a joke about nothing ever working right in big buildings like this, which her neighbor did not find amusing at all. She never invited my mother to go anywhere again.

When my mother asked her a few weeks later why she hadn't heard from her, even though they were right next door, the neighbor said, "You laugh at everything, and I didn't appreciate you laughing at me in front of the maintenance man when I needed something fixed." My mother was hurt, but she felt that the woman had no sense of humor.

So, I chose not to set my mother straight about her seemingly inappropriate enthusiasm about going onto hospice. I was glad that we had a plan, if it turned out to be necessary, and just a few hours later, it did.

Despite that plan and the preparation, I really sincerely hoped that the doctor would tell us that she just needed some different medication. I hoped that we'd be able to head to our new home in just two weeks, looking forward to day trips exploring the area, with my mother still somewhat independent and able to manage on her own. I imagined her walking easily around our house, helping to decorate and organize after the move.

I saw her preparing some meals, even if just for herself sometimes, and walking with me through markets and malls. But that's not what he said, and none of those things would happen.

He described her heart condition in easy to understand terms and he told us that she wasn't going to recover. When I asked him about hospice, he responded that her diagnosis would definitely be hospice appropriate and that he'd do a hospice referral for her, and he'd make that referral to a hospice in Maryland. I heard his words and, despite my preparation, I still felt myself sinking a little.

But my mother rose. She told him about Stella Maris, saying that we'd already found a place just in case, and I remember that he gave me a knowing look and a little smile. He was commending me for preparing her. But my mother's tone of gleefulness seemed to catch him off guard, and he laughed a little bit, nervously, as she was talking.

He said that he was glad to see that she was ready and willing, and he affirmed that hospice would be a good option for her, because she could take advantage of all the services. I think he was glad that he didn't have to convince her.

He took down the contact information for Stella Maris, and he told me that he'd make the referral before the end of the day, so that we could simply call and set up a home visit to start services when we got to the new house.

As we left, he hugged my mother because she'd been his loyal patient for years. He reminded her to use her walker, which she seemed to need almost all the time in those recent weeks, because her cane wasn't giving her enough support. We said goodbye to him, and I took her to the medical building lobby, where she sat on a chair and waited for me to bring the car.

When we got to her apartment building, we reversed that procedure, and I took her into the lobby and found a chair for her before going back outside to park the car. When I came back into the apartment building after parking, my mother was still sitting on that chair, but she was talking to one of the front desk workers, who looked very surprised.

As I approached them, the woman turned to me and said, "Your mother was just telling me that she got some great news today about going onto hospice care." Her facial expression told me that she'd need me to stop back at the front desk on my way out later on to clarify what the heck was going on. Who in the world would think that going onto hospice was *great news*?

Well, my mother would. And I was partially to blame for that cheerful attitude, given my persuasive conversation with her. But it did seem a little absurd, although it really was a relief to have her feeling okay about everything.

Before I left the parking lot of my mother's building after getting her settled back in her apartment, I sat in my still-parked car and called each of my sisters. I tried to explain as fully as possible what had happened that day, and they understood. It was hard for them being several states away, one north and one south. I think that either of them would have traded places with me to have more time with our mother.

There were plenty of times, especially yet to come, when I would have gladly made that trade. As we spoke, each of them wanted to call our mom later that evening, and I knew she'd appreciate that.

When I got home, I also talked to Scott, and then to Abby and Zoe, and I explained to them as well, what hospice would mean. I explained that my mother had a terminal illness, a heart condition that would likely be the cause of her eventual death, and that the hospice team would help to keep her comfortable while offering some support to us as well.

I told them, quite honestly, that having my mother referred to hospice just two weeks before our move would actually make things easier.

And it would also make things much harder.

To My Mother

What happened that made you
sometimes
choose Dad over me
even when he was blustering around
spewing ugly words?
Why did you say he was only
a little tipsy
while I remember the fear?
When you lessen his problem
you also lessen his achievement
when he stopped
when he came back to himself and
back to us fully.
It means nothing
if there was no problem.
But you stood between us
with your ever-present shield
defending me but also
defending him
from a child's outrage.
He has a temper, surely
that's true.
He doesn't mean it, but
of course, he does.
Your identity, his wife
and protector of family illusion,
even after things have healed.

Chapter 3
Unpacking It All

Scott: "I'm working on the home inspection report."
Mom: "They make good mayonnaise."

My husband, Scott, and my mother, Ellen, age 93

There were a lot of things to unpack, both literally and figuratively.

My memory of the first week in our new home consists mainly of cardboard boxes. Everywhere. It seemed inconceivable that all of this stuff would eventually fit easily into the house. When our Glenside home was packed up, it was a very cold January day, but by the time our furniture arrived in Maryland two days later, there had been a snowstorm.

Apparently, the furniture couldn't have been delivered on the day in between, because the moving company had contracted with local movers to unload the truck on a specific day, and no one was available a day early. So, the enormous moving van full of our furniture and beloved belongings sat at a truck stop near Exit 100 on Interstate 95 for two nights, while the driver and his work partner slept in the truck's cab.

Snow had to be shoveled in order to put down the rubber ramps to unload everything, and paths had to be created leading around to our back door too. Zoe had already gone back to college for her next semester, so Scott, Abby and I huddled in front of a space heater that the previous owners had left in the fireplace while the doors to our new house stood propped open for the movers. We stayed out of their way, but we had to be on hand for questions and instructions.

A week later, when it was time for my mother to move, we had made surprising progress in getting the boxes organized, if not unpacked. I drove up to Pennsylvania to get my mother, while Abby waited at the house in Maryland for my mother's movers to arrive with her things.

Her movers could make the trip and unload in the same day, because they were only moving a one-bedroom apartment, as opposed to our movers who moved a whole house-full of furnishings.

The drive to Maryland with my mother was actually quite lovely. I knew that she wouldn't like the highway, so I took Route 1 South all the way, past pretty countryside and through quaint towns. We saw horses and cows, and I know that she loved the scenic views. The drive reminded me of the hundreds of drives we had taken while I was growing up.

It was a regular habit for one of my parents to spontaneously suggest, 'Let's go for a ride!' on any given weekend. I have a vague memory of doing this with both of my sisters along, when I was little enough to be seated in the front seat between my parents in a red car seat that had a miniature steering wheel for me. It was more a plaything than a safety device. In those days, I'm fairly sure that we didn't even wear seatbelts.

As I was a little older and the rides were most often just me and my parents, I loved to curl up in the back seat with my face very close to the window glass, looking out as the scenery blew by. I'd stare deep into forests or out over farmland, with my imagination creating stories for the places we'd pass. I'd envision myself living or working in those places, maybe a princess lost in the enchanted woods, or a farmhand helping to care for beautiful horses.

Most often, we'd drive 'up the mountains' which meant a day trip to the Poconos. We had two restaurants that were our regular spots—Bradley's Bartonsville Inn and Terry's Italian Restaurant—and my parents knew the owners well at both places. We'd be greeted with smiles and handshakes, and the servers knew us too. My parents were so friendly, as well as loyal to these restaurants, that the owners probably loved seeing us come through the door.

Sometimes it would be our family of five, or sometimes my grandparents would be with us, but often it was just me and my mom and dad. As I got a little older, I was allowed to occasionally bring along a friend, and when someone else was with us, we'd have hilarious chatter during our car ride, with my dad telling outrageous stories and my mom being the perfect audience for him, laughing and trying to contribute some details, while he made fun of her too.

I remember one particularly raucous drive when we'd seen a lot of rocks by the roadside, and my father joked that they were my mother's homemade meatballs. He was able to embellish that one joke to make it last for a good length of the trip, with all the laughter at my mother's expense, even though he actually loved her meatballs. But I liked the quieter rides the best, the ones when I could just stare out the window as my parents talked quietly in the front seat.

I'd listen to the music from the car's radio, letting it carry me away, and sometimes I could convince my parents to put on pop music that had lyrics instead of their easy-listening instrumental jazz, which was my dad's pick. I remember that it was during those car rides when I first noticed that very often I'd be thinking about something, sort of praying about something, and the lyrics from the radio would address my question specifically.

Once, for example, when I was around fourteen years old, I was debating in my head about whether or not to go all by myself to visit my sister, who was married and living across the country. My parents had given me permission to fly alone, but I wasn't sure if I was too afraid to make the flight by myself. As I was thinking about it, I said a quiet prayer asking God or the Universe what I should do, and instantly the song on the radio switched and on came John Denver singing *Fly Away*. It seemed like magic to have such a specific response to my thoughts, and that kind of thing happened a lot on the car rides.

So, as I drove with my mother toward our new home in Maryland, I wasn't at all surprised to hear the songs that came onto the radio. I had my Sirius XM radio tuned to the Broadway channel, and during that drive we heard *Something's Coming* from *West Side Story*, *Home* from *Beauty and the Beast*, and *I Have Confidence* from *The Sound of Music*. The music itself was assuring me that things were going to be all right.

The music touched both of our hearts, because my love of Broadway show tunes came from my mother. I remember her laughing uncontrollably and mimicking Robert Goulet in *Camelot*, because although she adored that show, the song *If Ever I Would Leave You* struck her as hilarious for some reason, and I never figured out exactly why. She laughed equally hard at the *Stepsisters' Lament* from Rodgers and Hammerstein's *Cinderella*, after we watched the TV production starring Lesley Ann Warren.

My mother couldn't get over how amusing those stepsisters were, one with a creaky knee and one with batty eyelashes. We would dance around together to *Shall We Dance* from *The King and I*, singing and laughing, and because of the way my mother sang along emphasizing the rhythm of the music, I grew up thinking that the song was actually entitled 'Shall We Dance Boom-Boom-Boom'. I remembered those joyful times as we drove along together.

She was having a surprisingly good day and was comfortable in my car. My sister had gotten my mother ready and had helped as the movers arrived and got started packing that morning. By the time I got there, things were in full swing, and a priest who was one of my parents' closest friends even stopped by to give my mom a blessing and wish her well on her journey.

A little later, the movers had emptied the apartment, and we said goodbye to my sister who was about to head to the airport herself, and my mother and I were ready to begin our three hour road trip.

I had planned some stops along the way, in case she needed a break or a bathroom. We went to a Wawa market about a third of the way into our trip, and my mother was thrilled to get a milkshake and a Philly soft pretzel. It really didn't take much to make her so happy. She acted as though it was a gourmet treat, and I was relieved that the trip was off to such a good start.

Further along, as we continued into Maryland, we started to see signs for the town of Conowingo, and my mother got very excited.

"Are we going to see the Conowingo Dam?" she asked with all the eagerness of a child about to open Christmas presents.

"No," I teased, "we're not going to *see* it. We're about to drive over it!"

I knew that crossing the Susquehanna River by driving across the large hydroelectric dam was part of the route, but I had no idea that she'd be so delighted about it. She told me quickly and excitedly that she and my father had often seen the dam from farther down the river when driving on another road, but always in the distance and never up close. She was over the moon when we started to drive right across.

She sat forward, despite her seatbelt, and looked in all directions. It was by far the highlight of the day for her, and she talked about it for weeks afterward, telling everyone who called to check on her that she'd crossed the Conowingo Dam on her way to our new home.

It was equally special because that dam sits on the Susquehanna River, which my mother had always, for as long as I could remember, referred to as her own river. As she told us so often, she 'was born on the banks of the Susquehanna'. Although, I later learned that my grandmother gave birth in a house across the road from the river bank, with a midwife helping her through, I'd grown up thinking that my mother was literally born in the grass on the banks.

By the time she arrived at our new house, she was convinced that the move would be a positive experience. She felt that the drive itself proved that this was meant to be. She was especially delighted when Abby greeted us at the door, and Abby did a marvelous job of welcoming my mother and immediately showing her around the main floor of the house. Abby and my mother always had a special relationship, and having her attentive granddaughter there for the arrival made my mother so happy.

It also gave me a few minutes to take a breather after driving with my mother. Abby sat with her and was the first to hear the story of driving across the dam.

A few hours later, while my mother was comfortably seated in an armchair, her movers arrived with her things, including her upright piano. We had donated our own second-hand piano to a friend, because we preferred having my mother's piano in our house with so many family memories attached to it. That piano had been a gift to my mother from her parents when she was young, and it had always been in her home.

She was a phenomenal pianist. My sisters and I had taken piano lessons and practiced on that piano. More recently, Zoe often visited my mother in her apartment and played that piano while singing song after song for my mother. My mother had told me that she wanted Zoe to eventually inherit that piano, because she loved listening to her play and sing. My mother still played often too, and it was great exercise for her arthritic fingers.

As the piano and the boxes were carried into our house, we realized that my mother probably had more boxes per capita than the rest of us had. I'm not sure how all of that stuff had been in her apartment. We quite literally had boxes covering most of the floor space inside the house.

Over the next few days, I embarked on helping my mother unpack, which really meant that I'd pull items out of her boxes while she sat nearby and told me where things should go. Abby did a lot of the work too, and she seemed to take pleasure in helping my mother sort her things. Being super organized and always willing to help, Abby was invaluable for getting things out of boxes and into closets and drawers.

As we'd decided in advance, my mother could furnish and decorate the den and her upstairs bedroom, and we'd combine our belongings throughout the rest of the house.

Some of her items had minor damage from the move, and some were duplicates of things we already owned. So, there was a lot of discussion about what should land where in our new home. I felt myself tensing up because we had to pause from unpacking to talk about every single item as I pulled things out of boxes, as if she didn't trust me to put things away in a logical manner.

I felt like it was an indication of things yet to come, that she'd be trying to instruct and oversee my every move. I knew that these were her beloved objects, and she had always been very territorial about her belongings, but I just wanted to be trusted to unpack the boxes and to treat her things with respect.

But in fairness to her, I didn't treat everything with respect. She brought along some items that I simply didn't think were worth moving to a new home. Old pillows that were yellowing, blankets that had torn edges, knickknacks that were chipped, kitchen gadgets that she hadn't been able to use in years. I couldn't see the value in any of them.

I rolled my eyes as I placed them into the spots she indicated, and I resented that she'd brought all of this junk to our home. It wasn't until later that I realized that the sentimental value couldn't be seen. The pillows had been on my father's bed, and the blankets had been handed down to her by her own mother. The knickknacks and gadgets were hers when she had been able to use them and enjoy them.

These things had memories that were bigger than the boxes that held them, and my vision was blocked by the stress of trying to set up the house and, probably, by my resentment of her moving in with us. This wasn't what I had envisioned for my life.

There was more to unpack than the physical boxes. My relationship with my mother had become strained over the years, and I needed to recognize and understand what had happened and why. Zoe described my mother and me as magnets, saying that sometimes we seemed to repel each other whenever we got close, while at other times, with a bit of a turn, we connected and clung to each other.

My mother was my matron of honor when Scott and I got married. Partly, that was because it was impossible for me to choose between my two sisters, and partly it was because my mother was my best friend. I can't possibly count all the nights when my mother sat at my childhood bedside late into the night talking with me and reassuring me about everything in the world that frightened me. I told her about my life plans, my goals, my dreams. And she praised me and told me that I could do anything.

I told her about my friends and even about my romantic relationships with boyfriends. I always had to take the lead with those conversations, because she never seemed comfortable talking to me about anything remotely sexual in nature. In fact, when I first got my period, I was completely blindsided because I had no idea what was happening.

I thought something was wrong with me, that I was injured, and I remember that my mother called one of my older sisters to bring me a maxi-pad, which made me feel even more ignorant, because my sister obviously knew what was going on. And then, when I left the bathroom and went to lay on my bed, my mother gave me three thin little booklets, published by Playtex, one pink, one yellow and one pale blue, explaining how the female cycle works. The booklets had drawings of internal reproductive systems, male and female, and they also listed the mating habits of various animals.

I'm guessing that they were published in the 1950s, because they seemed old, even when she handed them to me. My mother told me to let her know if I had any questions, but I was too embarrassed to ask any, because I really wasn't sure what the point was. Honestly, I don't think I ever finished reading them, because they were boring and, honestly, a little disturbing.

I was completely sheltered and naïve. I gradually found out more practical information from my friends, and I pieced things together from innuendos on TV shows and in songs on the radio. That was a bit better than those booklets, but I went into adulthood feeling very uncertain about sex and most other things too.

Still, as I was growing up, I talked to my mother about boyfriends, the same way I'd talked with her about possibly becoming a nun. In fact, since I'd changed my mind about a religious life, I think I may have been trying to sell her on the greatness of these guys I dated. I wanted her to believe that I was going to find my true calling somewhere other than a convent, just like Maria in *The Sound of Music*. There were a few guys who really captured my heart as I grew up, and my mother knew all about them.

More than anything, I wanted my mother's approval. But really, I wanted her *enthusiastic* approval because I loved having her in my corner, telling me I was on the right track. I didn't want to disappoint her in any way.

It wasn't until I was in my early twenties that I stopped sharing with her about my dating life. I had been dating a guy that I was totally falling in love with and I'd told her that. Even though this guy hadn't said anything about it, I could see myself married to him one day. I told my mother that too, and she really liked him. He was Catholic and played several musical instruments and was very funny, not to mention good with my parents.

My father often glared at him, but my mother could talk with him like old friends. But one day, after dating him for many months, as he and I sat together on the sofa with his arm around me tightly just after we'd been kissing for a while, he told me that he'd decided to go into the seminary to become a Catholic priest. A celibate Catholic priest. I remember suddenly feeling like I couldn't breathe.

It was the same year that I was getting ready to leave for the Jesuit Volunteer Corps, so at least I could take some consolation in already having the perfect way to escape from this horrible disappointment.

But when I told my mother about it, about my heart being broken, her reaction was unthinkable to me. She was happy. She smiled and clapped her hands together and she said that he'd make a wonderful priest, and she told me that God obviously had big plans for him. I cried. Then, she tried to comfort me, but by continuing to tell me that I should see how this was such a wonderful thing.

She saw *God's plan*, as she called it, before she saw my crushed dreams. She put her enthusiasm for religion ahead of her enthusiasm for my happiness. I wanted her to cry with me and feel my heartbreak, but she just couldn't do it. This guy was choosing priesthood, and to her, that could only be a wonderful thing. My heart was just an unfortunate consequence, so she told me that it was my obligation to be supportive of him in this choice.

He'd be doing God's work, she said. Still being Catholic myself at that time, I thought that maybe she was right, and I wanted to do the good thing, the Godly thing, but I was conflicted and filled with despair. My mother didn't understand at all. I believe that in those moments, I began to realize that I couldn't tell my mother everything any more, and I don't think I ever talked with her in depth about my relationships again.

The same guy asked me out the following summer, when I had returned from the volunteer year in Washington State and after his first year in the seminary, and he acted as if nothing had changed between us, being completely romantic. Then, at the end of the evening, he informed me that it was sort of an experiment to see how he'd feel being with me again.

But thanks to our date, he had clarity. He was going back for his second year in the seminary. I told my mother that we'd gone out, but only as friends, and she was so delighted that we were staying in touch. The whole situation made me feel disgusted. Or disgusting. I wasn't exactly sure which.

A few years later, when I met and dated Scott, it overlapped with my moving out of my parents' house and into an apartment with a roommate, and then an apartment of my own. Scott and I dated for three years before getting engaged. We'd met while we were both working at the Archdiocese of Philadelphia, both in Catholic Social Services. I worked as a caseworker in the Senior Adult Services department, and Scott was the administrator of the Research and Planning department.

Scott was the only Jewish guy working in the building, as my father liked to point out. The first time I spoke to Scott was on the elevator in the Archdiocesan office building. I stepped into that elevator and he was the only other passenger. I told him that I liked his necktie.

I wasn't flirting but just making conversation. He thanked me and he said that he'd heard from a co-worker that I sang and played guitar at the recent Catholic Social Services mass for Christmas. He said that the co-worker told him I sounded good, and Scott told me that he sings and plays guitar too. I thanked him and that was that.

The next time we spoke, we were on the top floor of the building, where there was a cafeteria style restaurant for employees. It was early morning, before work hours began, and I was having coffee and a bagel with another caseworker. Scott walked up and asked if he could join us, which wasn't unusual for employees to do.

The three of us chatted and laughed, and it became a regular thing for us to meet in the mornings for breakfast, usually with other co-workers too. Scott and I often made eye contact when something funny was said, and we seemed to have a similar sarcastic sense of humor.

One day, I was early to work and I was the first at the table, and Scott joined me next, arriving second. I remember feeling a tiny bit nervous, since he was in a different department and more senior in his position than I was in mine. I wasn't sure it would feel okay to be alone with him for breakfast, but any awkwardness dissolved quickly and it wasn't long before we were laughing as usual. As the others arrived, I actually felt a little disappointed, because he and I were getting along so well.

A few weeks into our routine of morning coffee-talks, Scott invited me and another caseworker to go with him to a concert of the world famous Bulgarian

Women's Choir. My co-worker was familiar with them and thought it sounded great, and I loved choral music and thought it could be great fun to get together outside of the office. The concert was much more hip and contemporary than I'd expected, and we had a great time. It was obvious that we were becoming good friends. I honestly didn't have any ideas about dating him, until he asked me out.

The phone call from Scott came in April, on the day when I was throwing my middle sister's bridal shower at my parents' house. I answered the landline phone in the dining room, and was surprised to hear Scott's voice. He said that he knew it was the day of the shower, and he remembered me saying that I was stressed about it and hoping everything would go smoothly, and he wondered if I might want to get together later in the evening, after the shower was over.

He asked, "Do you want to dance or jam or something?" I remember that I was instantly intimidated about jamming with him, because by that time I knew that he had a band and wrote his own songs, and I was afraid that I wouldn't be able to keep up.

So, I replied, "Yeah, I could dance…!"

He picked me up and came inside to say hello to my parents and my sister, and then we went to a club on South Street in downtown Philadelphia to dance. Scott still talks about dancing with me that night to *Just Like Heaven* by The Cure, and he says that that's when he started to feel like this could really be something good. I remember feeling so completely relaxed with him, and feeling like I didn't have to pretend to be anything different than myself.

A week or so into our dating, we were watching TV at Scott's house, probably *Seinfeld* in its original run, when Scott asked me if I knew how old he was. I thought it was an odd question. So, I countered by asking him if he knew how old I was. He said that he knew I was twenty-five, and he again asked if I knew his age. I knew he was older than me, likely in his early thirties, so I guessed thirty-three. He was quiet for a moment.

"I'm forty," he said, and he looked at me as if he wondered if I'd be okay with that. I was a little surprised, because I didn't believe he was that much older than me. He didn't seem it.

"Well…Bye," I said, and I stood up.

He stared at me for a few seconds, and then I burst out laughing. For a moment, he thought that I was really leaving, and when he realized I was joking, he double-over laughing. Of course, his age didn't matter to me because we were having fun together and getting along so well. He never pressured me in any way.

Scott was truly the kindest person I'd ever met, and he also quickly became my most playful friend. We loved being silly together, and we both gradually came to realize that we would be spending our lives together.

We dated for three years before deciding to get married. There was no proposal, just a discussion at Rizzo's Pizza in Glenside. We had no idea that night that we'd eventually wind up living in Glenside, spending sixteen years raising daughters in a home we'd love so much. On that night, we talked about reasons that Scott didn't like engagements.

We talked through all the negative associations that Scott had with wedding planning, and we resolved to get married without all the fuss that can happen during the engagement process. We would handle all the planning ourselves, and we'd pay for the wedding ourselves too.

Scott's hesitation about engagements and weddings was completely understandable to me. He had been married before, at age twenty-one, and his first wife died young from cancer. He became her caregiver after her diagnosis. He often spoke about their engagement as a time when deposits were flying and things felt out of control, possibly because they were young and their parents were taking over.

At one point, Scott called off their wedding because he needed to slow things down for his own sanity, but they eventually got back on track and actually married sooner than originally planned. But the weekend of their wedding was tragic. Scott's father suffered a heart attack shortly before the wedding, and he died later that weekend. They cancelled their honeymoon and instead found themselves involved in funeral planning.

Scott, being six years older than his brother, was the one who actually went to the funeral home and picked out the casket, at a time when he should have been celebrating as a newlywed.

It made sense to me that he wanted to avoid those wedding associations, so I didn't expect a big proposal and a formal engagement. I just wanted to move forward with our life together and plan a marriage. We both knew that we belonged together.

When we made the decision to get married, my parents were the first people we told.

Scott and I went to their house, having called ahead to make sure they were available, and we sat in the bright florescent light of the kitchen to talk. My father sat at the head of the table, with my mother to his left and Scott to his right. I sat beside Scott and I think that I was more nervous that evening than ever before in my life.

Scott was the one who actually said the words, in a voice more formal than I'd ever heard him use. "Loretta and I would like to get married," he said, matter-of-factly. We knew that they wouldn't be happy, so we didn't delude ourselves into thinking we should present this gleefully.

My father's face turned white. Both of my parents sat completely still, not speaking. My mother looked at my father a few times, but said nothing. I honestly thought from the look on my father's face that he might have a stroke or a heart attack. The silence probably only lasted for a minute or two, but it felt like it dragged on, and I started to think I might faint. I had expected displeasure, but I didn't think it would be quite this painful.

Finally, my father spoke. "What are you going to do about children?"

I knew that he wasn't asking whether or not we intended to have children. He was asking how were going to raise them. He wanted to know what religion we'd choose.

Scott and I had talked about that so many times and we were prepared for this question, although I don't think I expected it to be the first words out of anyone's mouth when we announced our engagement. Scott and I took turns talking because we had resolved ourselves to stay focused and determined. We explained that we had decided to teach our children about both of our religions, Catholicism and Judaism.

Because I was already certified as a teacher of Catholic Religion from my master's degree studies, I was planning to teach religion at home. I had already been learning a lot about Jewish practices too, so we planned to give our hypothetical children instruction in both faith traditions.

"Will they be baptized?" My mother finally spoke. That was her first question, her first words on our engagement.

We assured her that any children we might have would be baptized, and they'd also have Hebrew naming ceremonies.

"What about the other sacraments?" She continued. I couldn't believe that we were already discussing my yet-to-be-conceived children's First Communion and Confirmation, when Scott and I were barely engaged. But I answered, saying that we had decided to teach our children about these faith traditions, taking one step at a time. My parents definitely were not satisfied.

The conversation probably wasn't as long as it seemed to me, and it didn't get any more pleasant. We told them that we had decided to keep the wedding very small, and we were planning to pay for everything ourselves. Basically, my parents took this as their opportunity to list their objections to me marrying Scott. They had three objections.

First, Scott was Jewish, and they wanted me to have children who would be raised Catholic. No amount of discussion was going to change that for them.

Second, Scott was almost fifteen years older than me. Scott and I had also talked that through, and we knew that we could make it work. In our hearts, we felt like we were the same age. In fact, Scott often seemed younger than me with his playful and silly nature. But my mother actually sat there at the kitchen table and said, "I know that this relationship seems glamorous to both of you..." which seemed ridiculous to me.

I couldn't help thinking that she didn't know us at all. Neither of us was anywhere near glamorous, and our age difference barely mattered to us. It certainly wasn't a point of attraction. We both knew that there might be challenges ahead regarding our ages, but *glamorous* didn't enter the picture at all. It was a curious argument from her.

And their third objection was that Scott had been married before. This objection caught me more off-guard than the others. How could they possibly object to him having been married, when his wife died of cancer after he took care of her for many months in their home? He was already proven to be a devoted and loving man, who cared for his wife until the end. Nothing could possibly be a greater testament to his character.

How was this possibly a negative? But my mother said that Scott was 'more worldly' than me because he'd been married.

At some point, Scott and I realized that we weren't going to make much more progress in appeasing them, and we'd told them what we needed to say. So, we said that we were going to head over to his mother's place to share our news with her, and we stood up to leave. They stayed seated at the table as we headed through the house toward the front door. My father didn't get up, but to her credit, my mother did get up and followed after us and caught us just before we left the house.

She didn't look especially happy, and in fact her facial expression looked like true pain, but she said, "I just want to say congratulations to you both," and she hugged us. It wasn't until years later that I realized how difficult that must have been for her, especially knowing that after we left, she'd have to go back to that kitchen where my father was still sitting at the table.

Two days later, my father called me while I was at work. He kept the conversation short and simple. He said that he'd thought about it and he decided that Scott and I should have an actual wedding with a celebration. He didn't think that we needed to keep it so small. It was his way of telling me that he would try to get past his objections. I had no idea what had changed for him, except that maybe he realized that we were going to get married with or without his approval.

Scott and I stuck with our plan to pay for everything ourselves, but we did eventually decide to have a bigger wedding than we initially intended, with a priest and a rabbi, and we designed the service ourselves to include parts of Catholic and Jewish ceremonies. Our friends and family gathered with us in a local country club for the ceremony and for a beautiful, happy reception. My parents celebrated with us. It was really amazing to see the change that had happened in those few months.

After just a handful of meetings, they had started to love my in-laws, and my mother seemed delighted to be my matron of honor. She had cried happy tears when I asked her. It was my way of offering some healing, trying to recapture the relationship that my mother and I had once had.

We kept our word about having both of our daughters baptized, and we also had Hebrew naming ceremonies. For each of our girls, we held the Catholic and the Jewish ceremonies on the same day, so our friends and family could witness both rituals. We went to the local parish church for the baptism, and then had the Hebrew naming a few hours later in our home.

We did that twice, two years apart, for Abby and then for Zoe. They each wound up with two sets of godparents, both Christian and Jewish. My parents seemed okay with all of it.

Still, we had our challenges over the years. When I was pregnant with Zoe, before we knew if I was carrying a girl or a boy, I told my parents one afternoon that the boy's name we'd chosen was Jake. My father became furious, and he hollered, "Why don't you just name him Mordechai?" I was shocked, and it took me several seconds to even process why he was so upset and what his outburst meant.

He was outraged because we'd chosen what he considered to be a Jewish name. He was angry and embarrassed that people might think his grandson was anything other than Catholic. There was so much wrong with his comment, I didn't know where to begin. I burst into tears and immediately stood up to leave their house. My father continued yelling, and he told me that he didn't know how he'd possibly tell his friends that he had a grandson with such a Jewish name.

He kept yelling at me and I couldn't stand it. I had to get out of there. Scott wasn't with me that day, so my mother walked me to the door, all the time trying to explain to me that my father only meant that he hoped we'd choose a name that was more expressive of *our* family too. I remember that I turned around, with tears streaming down my face and my hands resting on my pregnant belly, and I asked my father if he was interested in knowing why we chose that name.

I told my parents that we chose Jake to honor my mother's grandfather, whose name was Jakob. And if indeed we had a baby boy, the middle name we chose was going to honor my grandfather, Henry. So, both the first and the middle names were chosen for my side of the family, not Scott's, but my father had erupted before I'd even had a chance to tell them that. Frankly, I didn't feel that I needed to stick around that day to hear any more. My mother called me later that evening and she asked me to try to understand my father's point of view.

I couldn't and I didn't. And I also didn't understand how she could defend him, and how she could watch her pregnant daughter walk out of the house in tears, knowing I was about to get behind the wheel and drive my crying-self home, and still ask me to be more kind to him. It was another crack in our relationship, and it made me less likely to try to please them, although I still wished for their approval all the time.

I know that my parents were ultimately very disappointed, because when my daughters were old enough to be taught about religion, things changed for me. I tried to fulfil what I'd said that night when we were first engaged. I tried to teach my two little girls about Catholicism and Judaism. I purchased age appropriate workbooks and materials for both faith practices and I sat with Abby a couple of times a week gently guiding her through.

But as she asked more and more questions, my own doubts and questions came flooding back to me. I found that I simply could not, with any integrity, teach these two religious practices to my children. I disagreed with much of the dogma and some of the traditions, and I knew deep in my heart that while I would teach my children *about* these religions, as part of their heritage, I wouldn't raise them in either tradition.

Scott agreed completely, not being especially religious himself. For me, it was far more important that my daughters understood spirituality and could recognize the divine in our everyday world. We would guide them with strong values and principles, teaching them to be respectful of other religions, and trust them to find and develop their own worldviews as they progressed through life.

Eventually, I found Quakerism, and that faith and practice spoke to my heart. Based in Christian teachings but open to all beliefs, Quakerism focused on testimonies of simplicity, peace, integrity, community, equality, stewardship and service. There was no creed or clergy, and people sitting side by side could have different worldviews. What joined us together in a Quaker, or *Friends*, meeting for worship were two guiding principles.

The first is the belief that there is a Light within every person, and the second is called Continuing Revelation, which is the understanding that the revelation of the divine continues even in the present day, and that individuals can experience the divine directly.

I'd known a few Quakers over the years, and I also remembered learning about Quaker meetings in elementary school on a field trip to the Arch Street Meeting House in downtown Philadelphia. I remembered being intrigued by what I'd heard. Quakers worshiped in silence, and they were allowed to stand and speak when they felt led to share a Spirit filled message with those gathered. That memory of the simple practice stayed with me.

When I finally started attending Abington Friends Meeting, I felt like I'd found my spiritual home. I wanted Scott to try it out, and we brought our young daughters. Parents were invited to sit in on the Sunday classes for children, so Scott went with the girls to the class for the youngest Friends. He told me afterward that the teachers were reading a story about Jesus to the class, and one of the children asked, "Was Jesus really God?"

Scott said that the teacher replied, "Some people think so. Let's talk about that." And Scott was sold. He loved the idea that the children were being taught to embrace questions and explore all possibilities, rather than being told what to believe. We felt that we'd found a community where our little family would fit in.

I also understood that the Quaker faith and my family's approach to spirituality might not be appealing to everyone. I continue to respect that there are many paths to the divine in our universe, and I believe that the Creator can present different paths to different people. Yet, I was quite glad that we'd seemed to find one that worked for us.

We decided to raise them within the Quaker community, but we also wanted them to keep their Jewish identity through the celebration of holidays and other traditions. I didn't feel that same pull toward Catholicism.

My parents' dismay over our decision not to raise the girls as Catholics was constant.

They were also deeply wounded that I myself had left the Catholic Church. I completely understood and accepted that their religion worked well for them, but they simply could not reconcile my choice with their hopes for me and my children.

Despite all of that, we continued to have an extremely close relationship with my parents, both in physical distance and in quality time spent together. They were loving grandparents and my daughters grew up knowing them well. I'm not sure that my girls even realized until they were older how disappointed my parents were in my choices.

The girls didn't notice anything amiss when my mother would give them rosaries or Catholic prayer books, and I didn't really have an objection either, because it was part of their heritage, but it made me uneasy. My mother rarely spoke to me about religion, but it was always simmering just below the surface with her comments. She'd talk to me about Catholic holy days and traditions, as if it was taken for granted that I'd been thinking about those things.

In fairness, though, my parents embraced our nieces on Scott's side of the family and treated them almost as if they were grandchildren too. It didn't matter to my parents that those girls were Jewish, because their parents were both Jewish. The problem was that my parents never stopped seeing me as Catholic, which meant that my children—their grandchildren—should have been Catholic too. I never felt that my parents respected or even accepted the path we chose.

Yet, here we were unpacking boxes as my mother was moving into our house and fully into our daily lives. We were setting up her bedroom upstairs, her bathroom next to her bedroom, and her den on the first floor. Our lives were about to be entwined physically and emotionally, and I knew that we still had the biggest thing of all to unpack.

Possibly the most poorly timed and painful thing ever said to me was said by my mother.

It happened on the night that my father died. My father had lived for four years after receiving a diagnosis of stage four lung cancer. He had been through lengthy chemotherapy and radiation treatments, which exhausted him and left him feeling beaten up. He also had heart disease and melanomas on his skin. But he was a fighter, and by that point in his life, he'd turned things around so that he was enjoying these years knowing that he was nearing the end of his life.

I had been the regular driver for all of his appointments and treatments, and I'd assumed the tasks of taking my mother grocery shopping and helping her with all of their errands.

So, when my mother called me one night in February of 2009, just before midnight, to tell me that my father was having trouble breathing and wanted to go to the ER, it wasn't unusual. She told me that he wanted to assure me that he was fine, and he was getting himself dressed, but he felt that maybe he needed a breathing treatment or some suction or something to help him get some relief. She told me to take my time driving over to their house, because it didn't seem like a full-out emergency.

So, I got dressed and headed right over, planning to drive him to the ER myself, instead of calling an ambulance.

When I got to their house, my father was walking around and being his usual jokey self, laughing at my mother for trying to neatly roll up his oxygen cord so that he could switch to his portable unit. He went into the hall bathroom of their ranch house to comb his hair because he wanted to look nice at the ER, and he left the bathroom door open. A moment later, he started to call to my mother asking her to quickly bring back the oxygen. I heard in his tone of voice that he was starting to panic.

He really shouldn't have taken off the oxygen, but he wanted that final moment to tidy his hair while my mother switched tanks. When I saw his face in the bathroom mirror, I instinctively put my arms around him. He was a big guy, and he collapsed sideways into my arms, so I guided him to sit on the lid of the toilet seat. He looked at me with fear in his light blue eyes, and he couldn't speak. My mother quickly brought in the oxygen and I told her to call an ambulance.

She ran to the kitchen to make the call, and my father collapsed even further into my arms so that I was completely supporting his upper body weight as he leaned toward me. I sat on the edge of the bathtub so that we wouldn't fall to the floor. I held the oxygen cannula in his nose, because we hadn't had a chance to secure it around his ears.

My father stared into my eyes and I knew. The change had been so sudden in those few minutes, but the look in his eyes told me that he knew what was happening. I whispered to him that it was going to be okay. That he could let go, if he needed to.

"I'll take care of Mommy," I promised. And he slowly blinked his eyes because he was too weak to nod, and stared at me for a moment more. "I love you, Daddy," I said. "We'll be okay."

He closed his eyes and his head bobbed forward, and he let out one big, loud breath, almost like a rumble. He never opened his eyes again.

My mother came in a moment later saying that the ambulance was outside and that the medics were coming in. They squeezed into the small bathroom and I quickly told them that I wasn't sure if he was breathing. They asked my mother to step outside and then they somehow found a way to support my father's weight so that I could also step outside the bathroom too.

They didn't say much but they put my father onto a stretcher that resembled a tilted chair and took him into the ambulance, telling me where they were headed so that my mother and I could follow in my car. She was crying softly, but she spoke to him as he lay silently on the stretcher, before they put him into the ambulance.

I took her to my car and we followed the ambulance toward the hospital. After about three blocks, I realized that they hadn't put on the lights or sirens, so I turned off and took a parallel street, hoping that my mother wouldn't have the same realization just yet. I said that I thought the other street was quicker. My mother actually seemed relieved not to be directly behind the ambulance. And she asked me if I thought that he had died.

I said, "Maybe."

When we got to the hospital emergency room, the ambulance had just arrived and they were taking my father into a room. The nurse at the desk asked us to sit down in the waiting area. Just a couple of minutes later, a doctor approached us and invited us into a small side room. She told us, plainly and in very few words, that my father had died.

It was the saddest that I'd ever felt in my life, and my mother and I clung to each other. I remember thinking that I had to keep my arm around her because I was worried that she might faint. The doctor walked us to the room where we could be with my father, and she left us to have some time alone with him. My hands were shaking and I felt nauseous, but I was totally focused on my mother, because I knew he was her rock. I was afraid that she'd completely fall apart.

She walked toward him, with tears streaming down her face. I stood just behind her, holding her elbow as she reached out to touch his face. I cried too, and I hardly knew what to do with myself. It was a moment that I knew I'd never forget. And then, my mother turned around and looked at me.

"He hoped that he'd live long enough to see you come back to church," she said.

What? What did she just say?

I felt like I couldn't breathe. I could barely even process that those words had come out of her mouth. It was the first thing that she said after he died. The very first thing. She'd lost her husband and I'd lost my father, and her first words were about me not being Catholic. About me disappointing him. About me preventing his dying wish from coming true.

And it was too late anyway.

I'm not sure what I said in response, but I think I mumbled something about being content and at-home with my spiritual choices. It wasn't an adequate reply. I'm not even sure if an adequate reply could have existed in that moment.

So, I turned my focus to the tasks that needed to be done, including making calls on my cell phone to my sisters, to Scott, to our close friends, to a priest. I felt like I was in a fog, and not only because I'd lost my father, but because my mother had shattered me with those words. I stood by her side through all of it, and when the priest arrived and spoke with us and blessed my father's body, I felt numb.

Within a day or so, I realized that she must have rehearsed that phrase. She *must* have practiced it with my father. I felt sure that they had talked about ways to get me to return to church, and he may have even asked her to say those words to me whenever he died. I absolutely could not believe that she would have spontaneously thought of saying such a thing, that those words and that thought would have immediately popped into her head in that horrific moment. It must have been rehearsed.

In hindsight, I also see that those words had the opposite effect from what she intended. She, and possibly my father, thought that they'd shock me into returning to church, or shame me about having let my father down, maybe envisioning me returning to church to ask for forgiveness. I suppose they imagined me returning to church to honor my father.

That phrase was actually the primary thought in my mind for many days, even while dealing with the painful loss of my father. But as I continued to hear my mother's voice in my head saying those words, I knew that I didn't want anything to do with her church. I didn't want to be part of something that motivated her to such profound insensitivity, bordering on cruelty, at one of life's most powerful moments.

She turned the moment of my father's death into a moment of shame for me. She made it a moment to evangelize, when it should have been our time to comfort each other and mourn.

Months later, I talked about that moment and those words with a trusted friend who was also a former Catholic, and my friend said something that helped me to find forgiveness for my mother. My friend said, simply, "You know, she was trying to save your soul."

And I did know. That was probably true. My mother had spent her life believing that her religion had all the answers, and that if I had been raised Catholic and left the church, then I would be in mortal danger at the time of my own death. No wonder they practiced that phrase.

No wonder my mother used the moment of my father's death to try to say something that would shock me into returning.

My parents wanted to save me because they believed that I needed to be saved. And to me, that was the largest item of all, waiting to be unpacked.

Caregiver's Lament

Why would my mother want to live with me—
a girl who disappoints her?
Why wouldn't she choose
my sister
or my other sister,
who invited her
into their homes?
Maybe she expects to
see them in heaven.
But not me.
I won't be in
her heaven, she believes,
she has to save
my soul.
But I'll be somewhere else,
somewhere,
a place for us
where things you say matter,
and an age of love and kindness
will be dawning.
But until that day
I'll be right here
trying
to answer her prayers.

Chapter 4
Becoming Routine

Scott: "Sometimes on my way to work I see horses."
My mother: "Did you just say something about seahorses?"

My husband, Scott, and my mother, Ellen, age 93

We spent the last five months of my mother's life being together almost every single day, but of course we didn't realize that they were the last five months while we were in them. I might have done things differently if I'd had a glimpse of the future and the timeline. If I'd known that we were counting down, and that she wasn't going to be one of those hospice patients who holds on for years, then I might have felt more patience and less frustration at her constant presence.

I'm not proud of my frustration but I don't think I could have avoided it. I'm human after all.

The hospice team from Stella Maris was in place two days after my mother moved into our new house. A nurse came for the evaluation visit and I had to clear a path through the boxes so that we could sit at the kitchen table together. The nurse told us that my mother was 'in great shape for a hospice patient' and that she expected that my mother could have 'quite some time' in their care.

My mother told the nurse all about her connection to the Sisters of Mercy, and as I'd expected, she asked the nurse if she was a nun. She wasn't. But she talked and joked with my mother, having a lovely conversation. My mother even told her about driving across the Conowingo Dam. The very next day, the regular hospice visits began. My mother was very pleased.

With those initial exams and evaluations of her vital signs, I was surprised to learn that my mother should not be left alone. I hadn't been planning to leave her in the house for any long period of time, but I had thought that I'd be able to run out to do an errand once in a while.

Before we moved, she had been living independently, but the nurses explained that my mother's heart was unpredictable. She might experience sudden weakness or dizziness if her heartrate dropped, so she needed someone to be nearby at all times. They also told me to be prepared that she might start to become confused at times, when her brain wasn't getting enough oxygen because her heart wasn't pumping well.

It was hard to imagine my mother being confused. Her memory was as sharp as a tack. Just a year or so earlier, my mother and I, along with Abby, had visited a cousin at his home in the Pocono Mountains. We hadn't seen him in many years but I'd reconnected with him on social media.

We planned the trip carefully, knowing that my mother would need to stop and stretch her legs halfway through the two-hour drive, and it felt like a fun adventure. The scenery was lovely as we drove north, and we were all excited about reconnecting with our cousin, who was around my age. His mother had been one of my mother's first cousins, and they had been raised closely. My mother's cousins were like her siblings because she was an only child, but the cousins all lived fairly close to each other and saw each other often as they grew up.

So, when my cousin brought out photo albums and family videos, my mother loved seeing them. My mother was the last surviving cousin of her generation, so she was the one to answer any lingering questions about family history and to fill in details about childhood memories. And she did it splendidly. My cousin was surprised and thrilled at some of the information that my mother was able to clarify, and he said that he could hardly believe how well she remembered even the tiniest details.

She shared with him stories about his mother, and stories about the generations before that. We spent the afternoon on his deck looking at the beautiful woods while my mother painted spoken pictures of our family history for us to absorb and remember. Yes, her memory was sharp and vivid.

The idea that my mother couldn't be left alone hit me like a punch. We'd just moved to a new neighborhood in a new state and I wouldn't be able to explore. Scott and I would have to take turns leaving the house. Abby was helpful during the first few weeks, but she accepted a job in Salt Lake City a month after our move, so she would be moving away, and Zoe was off at college.

But before Abby left for Utah, we did some initial drives around the area to see what was nearby, and we had the great luck to discover that our suburban neighborhood was very near some horse farms and beautiful countryside. So, as we settled into our new home, I often bundled my mother in her warm coat and took her carefully to my car to go on drives. We didn't ever go far, in case she started to feel unwell or needed to get home quickly, but we could usually drive for about an hour in giant loops around the scenic Maryland roads.

I think that those rides were my mother's favorite thing to do, and whenever she'd ask to go for a drive, I tried to accommodate. I do remember that there were times when I was busy with work and I couldn't just put things aside to go driving, but when she'd ask, I'd usually try to find time within the next day or so to take my mother out. There was only one time that I gave her an absolute 'No' about going for a drive, and it broke my heart to do it.

But she was not in good shape and I didn't even think that she could walk to the car, so I told her that we'd go when she felt better. And that was the week before she died.

Other than our occasional rides, we basically stayed in the house. More than we realized at the time of purchase, our new house perfectly suited my mother's needs, as well as my own and my family's needs. My mother had space to enjoy her belongings, and there was enough room for me to set up my laptop to work in a different room with a little bit of distance between us. Usually I worked in the dining room, so that she was not far away when she sat in her den, and I could hear her if she needed something.

I had the luxury of working from home, and it was a miracle that things with my job had worked out the way they did. At the time of our move, I had been working for eleven years at the Quaker meetinghouse. I was both a member of the Abington Friends Meeting community and also an employee. I had been asked to consider the job when my kids were little, and it seemed like the perfect part-time job.

I'd been a stay-at-home mom for a few years and then I took jobs teaching preschool, working in the local junior high school cafeteria, and eventually substitute teaching for our school district. So, the meetinghouse job seemed perfect for me. I took the job and became one of two employees, just myself in the office and the live-in caretaker, who did his work throughout all the buildings and grounds. My part-time job eventually grew, adding more hours each year, as the people in the Meeting community realized that I had some useful skills.

Eventually, my job became full-time and I became the administrator and bookkeeper. I honestly loved my job, because the work was constantly changing as I assisted about fifteen standing committees with their varied work, and the community was very supportive to me as an employee. I enjoyed that pastoral aspect and the religious setting, feeling that my training had prepared me well for this job.

When we decided to move in order to accommodate Scott's new job, I was truly heartbroken about having to leave the meetinghouse job, but being a non-profit organization, it didn't pay well enough to take precedence over the outstanding new opportunity for Scott. I figured that I'd look for a new job in Maryland. I gave as much notice as possible so that I could help to train someone to replace me, so they knew in October that I'd be leaving in January.

My job was supervised by a committee of volunteers, and at first they worked with me to figure out ways that I might be able to ease the transition for the incoming employee by continuing to do some of the more critical tasks remotely, until the new person would be fully trained. But it became apparent during the planning that much of the work I did could be handled remotely.

The committee asked me if I'd consider continuing to work remotely part-time, and they'd search for another part-time employee to handle the tasks that needed to be done on-site. So, another Meeting member was hired part-time, and we started to job-share what had been my full-time job. I was thrilled to be able to continue and to stay connected.

By the time we were actually moving, and we had found out that my mother had a hospice diagnosis, I realized how phenomenal it was that I would be working from home, and only for part of each day. I'd be able to care for my mother and work in between doing things for her. And because I'd be working remotely, I could work in the evening when Scott was home to be with my mother, or on the weekends. It seemed like another piece of this puzzle that had simply fallen into place to make conditions ideal.

I became acutely aware of our family's privilege during those early days in Maryland. So many people have so little and cannot hope to get by, but we were going to be able to manage, because we had what we needed. Being white and middle class, we had the luxury of resources. It was all privilege. I felt selfish for complaining about anything because we had landed in a house that had enough space for our needs.

If we had stayed in our Glenside house, which was a split-level with steps everywhere, I could not have brought my mother into our home. There was no first floor bathroom in Glenside and the multiple staircases would have been dangerous for her. But here in Maryland, the house was perfect and had everything we'd need. We also had the resources to be able to keep my mother at home with us.

Having in-home hospice care was a privilege, and having support and the means to get help was another privilege. And we were fortunate to have had enough education to know how to ask the right questions. I understood that I hadn't earned all of this. It had been handed to me. I knew that, and I felt grateful and guilty at the same time.

I also realized that despite our differences, I was also privileged to have been raised by loving parents who provided care and kindness, as well as the necessities of life, with many extras that so many people cannot afford or do not have access to. My mother, especially, did everything she could to ensure that my sisters and I would have well-rounded lives, with cultural and artistic experiences, and as much education as possible.

I felt ashamed of myself for holding onto resentment toward my mother who had given me so much, so the internal conflict of being her caregiver was a constant battle for me.

As the hospice workers started to visit on a regular schedule, I felt like I was making new friends. My mother's nurse initially came twice a week. In addition to providing care for my mother, she looked through our house and made recommendations for ways to make things easier for my mother. Within that first week, I'd found a local medical equipment store and I was purchasing elevated toilet seats with armrest-handles, adult size bibs so that my mother could take meals in bed, if needed, and nightlights.

The hospice supplied a wheelchair, to be saved until needed, a shower chair, and a commode, which my mother, quite proudly, never had to use. The commode became the place where we stacked her clean towels.

They also gave us an oxygen tank and a concentrator machine and trained me on how to use them, but my mother flatly refused to ever use oxygen. I'm not sure if it scared her because she knew that oxygen is flammable, or if she just had a negative association from handling my father's oxygen for so long. But she was adamant about not wanting to have 'those tubes' on her face, and I tried to respect her wishes about that, even when I absolutely knew that it would have helped her.

I tried frequently to change her mind about the oxygen, and my sisters often talked to her about it on the phone encouraging her to try it, but she stood firm.

She did not want to ever use oxygen. The nice thing about hospice is that they respect the patient's wishes. For whatever reason my mother may have had to refuse using oxygen, they wouldn't force her. Her care was under her own control, and they wanted her to be comfortable, both physically and emotionally.

Still, while the oxygen was stored in our house, the instructions said that we were required to place a sign in the window of each room where the tank or concentrator would be kept. It was supposed to be for fire safety and to warn about not smoking. My mother was aware that if firefighters ever had to come to our home, the rooms with oxygen would be marked from the outside by those signs, so she was extremely worried that her bedroom and den were ready to explode at any moment.

She really disliked those signs and all that they represented. In addition to being afraid of explosions, no matter how often I told her that there was really no danger, she also felt embarrassed by the signs. They seemed to remind her that she was supposed to be using oxygen, and she had no intention of doing that. She was so upset by the signs that I tried to place them in the windows in a way that the curtains would hide the signs from my mother's view.

The other issue that my mother's nurse advised us about was the staircase. I'd expected to have a lengthy discussion, assuming that we'd need to install a chair lift, because we had a full flight of stairs between our first floor and second floor, so my mother would have to walk up and down to get to and from her bedroom. But the nurse knew exactly what was to be done, and she made it very simple. It would benefit my mother to walk the stairs as long as she was able to. It would be good for her circulation and strength.

The nurse said that we should not get a chair lift, because if my mother got dizzy or confused, she could have an accident with that type of equipment. While chair lifts were helpful to some people, it wasn't the right choice for my mother, she advised. My mother might misjudge and think that she could handle it alone, or she might fall trying to get into the chair by herself. The nurse said that eventually, when the stair climbing became too much for my mother to handle, we'd have a hospital bed delivered to our house.

At that point, my mother would sleep in the den and she'd have the small bathroom right nearby. My mother wasn't happy about that scenario, but it seemed far off in the future, because my mother was still fairly mobile. Until that hospital bed became necessary, the nurse told me to simply stay a few steps below my mother every time she needed to go up or down the stairs, keeping my hand on her back for support, which is exactly what we did.

Several times a day, if she wanted something from her bedroom, or if she just wanted a change of scenery, I'd walk my mother up the stairs.

The social worker came as needed, less frequently than the nurse. During her first visit, my mother told her that she was incredibly beautiful, and she also said that the color of her sweater—royal blue—was the perfect color for her. She went on about it a little longer than necessary. The social worker seemed amused and thanked my mother for the kind words. My mother took a lot of joy in complimenting people, even when it seemed borderline inappropriate.

The social worker helped us with all the paperwork that was needed for my mother's Maryland healthcare. She advised me on how to update my mother's Social Security information and how to navigate Medicare. There were also advance directives, specific to Maryland, and paperwork about my mother's wishes for her time of death that needed to be completed.

There were days when I thought the phone calls were endless, and I had the added pressure of always having my mother by my side when I'd make calls on her behalf. I wanted her to be aware of exactly what was happening, and she appreciated being involved. But the calls took longer when I had to explain everything to my mother. She had never used a computer or a cell phone, and technology made her very nervous, so I was constantly assuring her that email and scanning things would be okay.

The social worker also advised us to pre-pay for funeral arrangements. She said that it would make things infinitely easier when the time came. Because my mother had mentioned that she would eventually be interred in the same grave plot as my father in Pennsylvania, the social worker encouraged us to work out those details of transport in advance. But she really didn't need to convince us.

My mother had been planning her own funeral for ten full years, since my father had died. It was actually her favorite pastime, and I'm completely serious about that.

For years, my mother took great pleasure in planning all the aspects of her funeral. She thought that my father's funeral turned out beautifully and the services had exactly the tone that she wanted, to honor his memory. So, of course, she wanted something very similar for herself. She selected the same music and the same readings, with only slight variations. It would be sort of like the companion funeral to my dad's.

Within months after his funeral, she had started to make lists of all the details for her own funeral. She jumped into that planning the way a bride might enthusiastically plan a wedding, and she always seemed especially happy when we'd talk about it.

At least once every month or so, she'd call me to her apartment to sit with her at the table and review every single detail. She had a list with the order of the program for the funeral mass, and she also had photocopies of the scripture readings stapled to the list. The list was in a folder, along with all the sheet music for every song and response that would happen during the mass.

The program list had been typed on her old manual typewriter, but she added handwritten notes in the margins, clarifying anything that might be in question. She put names next to each item, so that I'd know exactly who should be handling each part.

I often felt impatient when she'd insist that it was time to review her funeral plans yet again, because it was tedious and, I thought, unnecessary. I also didn't really like having so much emphasis on her funeral, despite her enjoyment of the discussions. She would also tell me fairly often not to talk about all of this with my sisters, unless they asked, because she didn't want to upset them by making *them* think about her funeral.

Wow. Okay, Mom. Thanks.

Often, when we'd sit together going over her plans, I didn't notice anything new. But sometimes she would have changed things around a bit, especially reassigning the roles that she wanted family members to have. Each of her grandchildren would have a special part in the funeral mass, and each of us daughters would also be involved. But she changed her mind a lot and rearranged things.

She would ask me questions, such as, "Do you think it would be okay to have all the granddaughters do the readings and psalms, and have the boys bring up the offertory gifts? Or should the boys be asked to read too? Should I mix it up?" Sometimes, she made it sound like we were planning a performance. Zoe was studying to become a professional actor and singer, and so my mother emphasized that Zoe should sing the responsorial psalm at the funeral mass.

My mother had been a huge supporter of Zoe's shows over the years, taking all the pride that can be expected from a grandmother, but it still struck me as funny when she'd look at her funeral program and say, "…and, here's the part where we'll have Zoe sing." It sounded like she was planning a show.

She chose pall bearers, and those were all male, including her three sons-in-law and two grandsons, and she also made a list of alternate pall bearers, just in case anyone on the A-List had any health concerns and couldn't lift a casket, whenever the time would come. She emphasized to me, both in person and in the notes on her paper list, that she didn't want any of this 'new-fangled stuff' of having female pall bearers. She couldn't wrap her brain around something as way-out as females carrying a casket, even though we definitely have women in the family who would have wanted to do that.

We talked about her funeral so often that I started to have things memorized. And she changed her mind so often about the little details that her corrections started to appear in different colors of ink, with arrows drawn to show which items were the most recent changes. She started adding extra pages, with notes to turn over the page, as things were listed on both sides.

She also kept a calling list, with names and phone numbers, for everyone who should be contacted whenever she died. That list, too, had cross-outs and scribbles, and because it was on yellow legal-size paper, the white correction fluid all over the page looked remarkably vivid.

Eventually, the folder grew to become a plastic bag filled with several folders. She had a giant rubber band around the bag to keep everything inside secure. Pages were stapled and paper-clipped together, and she started to add items. She had a lipstick in a baggie, which was supposed to be given to the funeral director.

She had a photo of herself, also to be given to the funeral director, because she wanted her hair to be done that same way. She also noted that I should ask the funeral director to please make her 'smile a little bit' in the casket.

Sure! Why not seem happy to be there?

She also selected what she wanted to be wearing in the casket. Unfortunately for me, she chose the gown that she wore to my wedding as her garment for burial. I couldn't argue, though, because she told me that she felt 'more beautiful on that day' than she had since her own wedding. So, I tried to hold onto that happy feeling, knowing that the dress had such good memories for her.

The underwear that she wanted to be wearing was in a plastic bag attached to the hanger with her gown, and she kept these things in the front of her closet so that I'd be able to grab them easily when her time would come. She also had a bag with flat black canvas shoes attached to that hanger, and I asked her once if she wouldn't rather have her fancier shoes to go with that formal gown. She replied, "I thought about being buried in those dressy shoes, but they're really not comfortable."

Umm, okay. I refrained from pointing out that she'd be dead when she had those shoes on.

It was clear in our many conversations that my mother envisioned herself being present at her own funeral. She asked questions like, "Where do you think we should go for the luncheon?"

And I'd reply, "Are you planning to be there?" Or, "I don't know. What do you think you'll want to eat that day?" She'd roar with laughter, realizing her mistake, and we actually had quite a lot of fun imagining different scenarios. At one point, I jokingly threatened to have her propped up in the corner of the room so that she could wave to family and friends, since she kept including herself in the count.

She thought that was hilariously funny and acted as if she might really consider that. But she made it clear, although she said it in a comical way, that she fully intended to be present with us, in spirit.

So, when it came to planning my mother's funeral from our new Maryland home, we were way ahead of the game. I contacted the funeral director that my mother preferred back in Pennsylvania, and we got instructions on exactly how to connect with them whenever my mother would pass. We were to contact a specific funeral home near us, and they would arrange the transportation. The funeral arrangements were made for everything to take place in Pennsylvania, and my mother and I spent several days with phone calls back and forth, setting up the plans exactly as she wished.

Everything was pre-paid and she approved every detail. She chose the casket she wanted, and she asked to be buried holding a rosary and five roses in her hands. The roses were to be three pink ones, representing me and my sisters, and two white ones, representing the babies that she had miscarried.

My mother also had a home health aide who came in three times a week to help her shower and wash her hair. My mother's showers had to be done in the bathroom that Scott and I used, which was connected to our own bedroom, because we had a stall shower. It was extremely difficult for my mother to step into a tub shower, so of course we readily agreed to using our bathroom as the place for my mother's time with her aide, a few times a week.

On the very first visit when my mother got her first shower in our bathroom, the water had splattered out onto the floor and onto the counter by the sink, and my mother's waiting pile of clean clothes got damp.

The aide called to me and asked me to bring something dry, as my mother was about to step out of the shower. I grabbed the closest garment I could find, because I didn't want my mother to be cold, and that was my own thick terry robe, hanging on the bathroom door. It had been a gift from Scott, and it was warm and cozy. My mother thought so too, and I never got it back. It became her regular shower robe because she enjoyed it so much.

After each shower, the aide would spend time talking with my mother as she combed and blew dry my mother's hair. She was extremely kind to my mother and very professional. She also always took a moment to chat with me, and I felt like she could easily become a friend if we weren't in this hospice-caregiver relationship. My mother always made a point of thanking her profusely, even though she usually did it using the wrong name.

My mother seemed to have a mental block when it came to remembering the names of the hospice workers, but she did recognize that this woman was taking care of her most personal needs, and the two of them would chat away as this kindly aide helped her get dressed and fixed her hair. The aide was busy from the moment she'd arrive at our house, but she'd always take just a minute to sit down as she filled out her paperwork, and she'd tell my mother that she had enjoyed their time together. She was an angel, and without her assistance for my mother, I probably would have lost my mind.

Her visits gave me a little bit of time to go outside for a quick walk or to run an errand.

We also loved the chaplain, who would come to see my mother a few times a month. She wasn't Catholic, but she showed interest in my mother's faith, and the two of them would have lengthy talks about theology and rituals and various practices. I would sit with them sometimes, but usually I took the opportunity to do some uninterrupted work in another room.

A few times, I overheard my mother explaining to her the Rite of Christian Initiation for Adults, or RCIA, which is the program for adults who wish to convert to Catholicism. My mother and father had been extremely active in the RCIA programs at their home parishes in Pennsylvania, and I wondered if my mother had a secret hope that maybe the chaplain would be interested in becoming Catholic too.

The chaplain sometimes asked my mother if she was 'seeing' any loved ones who had already passed away. I remember that my mother answered with no hesitation at all, saying that she saw them frequently and spoke to them too.

So, we started to settle into our new home with a caring team of professionals visiting several times a week, helping us to cope with all the changes that we'd experienced both with moving and with my mother's sudden diagnosis. I also knew that this team would be invaluable with all that was yet to come.

As our boxes were gradually disappearing, our home was filling up with my own anxiety.

It was clear that caregiving for my mother was about to become my full-time job. I might have part-time employment in an actual paying job, but my mother's care was going to be my primary focus. It felt remarkably similar to how I felt when my daughters were little. I felt myself shifting back to the mindset I had when I was taking care of them.

There wasn't going to be much free time to do things for myself. I had enjoyed being the caregiver the first time around, when my daughters were the ones pulling my attention. But I didn't know what to expect as I was starting to mother to my own mother.

The routine of our daily living together was beginning. And I had no idea how long this would continue.

Dusty

I used to write for no reason or
for every reason without thinking about
other people's art. Absorbed now
in mediocrity, like F. Murray Abraham in Amedeus,
I hum without words.
No lyrics for lunch boxes, no stanzas about
Slim-Fast and Girl Scout meetings.
I dust the bookshelves
of Ignatow, Pastan, Plath, noticing
bookmarks I left.
I touch them and
their words fall out, cluttering up my floor,
more toys at my feet, reminders of
somebody else at play.
I could easily pick up the
words, gather them up
off the floor and
sort them out, but the afternoon is
almost over, and I still have to vacuum.

Chapter 5
Life with My Mother

My mother has a substitute aide…
Mom: "Did you say your name is Alice or Anne?"
Aide: "Anne."
Mom: "Okay, Alice! That's what I thought."

My mother, Ellen, age 93

During the year that I lived in Washington State working on the Colville Reservation, my mother came to visit me for a week. I was there for a year and she was only there for a week. But she talked about that place for the rest of her life, as if she'd lived there herself. Of course, we'd had a wonderful week, exploring different parts of Washington, and even British Columbia.

We drove through the North Cascades, stopping at Liberty Bell pass, to see little towns that attracted tourists with Western and Alpine themes. And we went for walks around the high desert of north central Washington, enjoying some walking trails through the rugged landscape. We even visited a candy factory. She befriended a few of my friends during that week, and she continued to correspond with them for the rest of her life, as I did.

It was certainly a memorable week, and I tried to pack it with activities for her. And by doing that, I invited her to claim that beautiful place as her own. It had been mine, my adventure, but it also became hers.

I see now that our lives were always intertwined like that. Maybe it's that way for many parents. They take on the experiences of their children as their own. I certainly feel that way with my daughters and their adventures sometimes. I live vicariously whenever they tell me about things going on in their lives.

For most of my life, I loved having that connection with my mother. I wanted to share everything with her, and I wanted her to love the things I loved. And to my delight, she usually did.

It wasn't until the adult tensions and disagreements began that I started to want some distance from her. It just wasn't pleasant to spend time with someone who thinks I've made poor choices and who is trying to convince me to change my spiritual path. I was constantly aware of that judgment, that sense that things weren't quite right. My mother definitely gave off the vibe that she knew better, that she could fix things for me, if I'd only listen to her.

But here we were under the same roof, where distance and privacy were impossible. She noticed everything. I remember that she even reprimanded me one day for running up the steps too quickly. I'd been going upstairs for something that she needed from her bedroom, and I took the steps at a jog. "Don't you ever run up the steps like that!" She lambasted me as soon as I returned.

"I heard the way you ran up those steps, and you're going to fall and hurt yourself if you do that!" I tried to explain that I was fine and that I didn't mind the exercise, but she persisted. "You're going to fall down the steps if you run like that. I don't want you to do that again!" She just couldn't see me as an adult.

She rarely let things go when she had an opinion to express. But we had to work through it. We had to find a way to live together in some kind of dissonant harmony.

It wasn't long before our routine together became, well, routine. I'd start each day by checking to see if she was awake. Her bedroom was down the hall from ours, and when we moved our furniture into the house, I deliberately positioned our bed so that I'd be able to lean over from my side and see down the hallway to my mother's bedroom doorway. She kept her door almost all the way closed, so I'd be able to see if she'd gotten up by herself and opened it, and I'd also be able to see if her bedside light came on during the night.

In the mornings, I could tell when she was up, because I'd see a rose-colored light shining under her door. Her window had rose-colored curtains, and after she'd open the shade, the morning sunshine would pour in through that window dressing. I thought that it was an appropriate metaphor for my mother to be looking out at the world through a rose-colored window.

During the first couple of months, she often woke up early and sat looking out that bedroom window. We gave her the largest bedroom, besides our master bedroom, so she had a big double closet and plenty of room for her bedroom furniture and a chair. Eventually, we moved the chair out of the room when she needed more space to navigate with her walker, but she could still sit on the foot end of her bed and look out at the back yard.

The back of our house faced the woods and she loved looking out at the evergreens and the variety of leafy trees. She was especially fond of birds, so she enjoyed watching the many cardinals, blue jays, and even black vultures that frequently flew around nearby. Her window faced east, so she could often see the colorful sunrise over the trees.

I would tap on her door and come into her room whenever I knew that she was awake, and I'd always give her a cheerful, "Good morning!" because I knew she loved that.

She'd reply, "There's my good friend!"

I'd kiss her on the cheek, and she would reach up with her shaky hands to hug me and pat me on the back as I leaned in. So, our days almost always started off happily, and I'm glad about that.

I'd help her get to the bathroom, if she hadn't already gotten there by herself. I'd wait for her in her room and straighten her bed, which had to be perfect or she'd redo it herself when she returned from the bathroom, slowly walking around the bed, leaning over and holding onto the bed for support as she painstakingly removed every wrinkle from the sheets and blankets.

I'd have to stand there and watch because she didn't want my help, since I hadn't done it correctly in the first place. But I learned quickly how to make that bed the way she liked it, because it was too tedious to wait there each morning, watching her trying to fix my mistakes.

As soon as the bed was straightened, I'd help her get dressed. At first, I was helping her only because she would feel stiff or get winded, but eventually it became apparent that she was simply too weak to manage the task of dressing herself. I'd gone through her clothes when we unpacked the boxes, and I kept the softest pants and shirts in one spot so that I could easily grab those. Usually, she'd have me pull out an outfit at bedtime and fold her clothes on the dresser, so that everything would be ready and waiting in the morning.

I had suggested that she switch to soft, comfy camisoles under her shirts, and I bought her a few in white and beige. She loved those camisoles and she told me that I was a genius for buying them and for replacing "all those uncomfortable things with hooks and wires." She had a drawer full of white cotton socks, and although she also had many pairs of flat shoes, I bought her two pairs of moccasins that became her everyday footwear. She liked that they were soft, but they also had 'grippy soles'.

I chuckled almost every time I opened her closet, because my mother had more short-sleeved, floral print, pastel colored polo shirts than I've ever seen in one place. She kept them on hangers all in a row. She told me that she had ordered them from catalogues over the years. I suspected that she may have occasionally forgotten how many she already had.

Unfortunately, by the time my mother lived with us, her heart was already making her so frail, that she was almost always chilly, so she never wore any of those short-sleeved polo shirts while she lived with us. She had also started to feel that collars bothered her neck, so we had five or six collarless long-sleeved shirts that became her standards.

She also had two soft jackets, which I called *blazers* just to sound fancy and make her laugh, that were made from sweatshirt material and had snaps up the front. One was tan and one was turquoise, and she alternated them every day. She'd fill the pockets with tissues to be prepared for the day. I'd have to remove the tissues from the pockets every night.

Whenever I did her laundry, I had to fold her clothes immediately before they wrinkled, because if she saw wrinkles on her clothes, she'd ask me to iron them. She even wanted her nightgowns ironed. I did that twice, I think, before I just caught on about folding things more quickly. Of course, she offered to do the ironing herself, and she was completely serious about that, but I couldn't imagine letting her hold a hot iron in her shaky hands.

After she was dressed, sometimes she'd want to sit in her room for a few more minutes saying her morning prayers. When she insisted on doing that in her room, I'd go back downstairs to the dining room table and do some work for my job. She'd call to me when she was finished, and I'd sprint back up the steps to help her come down. Sometimes, she'd already be standing in the hallway with her walker, smiling and laughing because she would say, "Oh, good morning!" again, as if she was seeing me for the first time that day.

She cracked herself up. I just wanted to get up there quick enough to prevent her from getting too close to the top of the stairs. She was very unsteady and I didn't want any accidents.

I was relieved when I was able to convince her to start saying her morning prayers in the den, so that I could bring her downstairs a little sooner and get back to work with less interruptions. I'd walk her down the stairs and then get her settled in my father's old green recliner, which was getting a bit worn out by this point. She had a little table next to the chair to her left, and on her right side, she could reach out her right hand while seated to take things from her large bookshelves.

So, we kept her prayer books and prayer cards, which were all loosely rubber-banded together, on the closest shelf. She'd get settled in the big chair and then reach for them to begin. After about fifteen or twenty minutes, she'd call me, and we'd walk around the corner to her special seat at the kitchen table for breakfast.

That kitchen table and its six chairs had been hers before we moved, but it fit perfectly into our new kitchen. The tan and brown tones in the Formica table top and the dark brown chairs exactly complimented our pale beige kitchen. She was delighted that we could fit it into our kitchen, because she loved that table. I did too. It reminded me of my childhood, the good and the bad, in the rowhome in Northeast Philly where our family of five would sit together for meals and conversations, for late night pizza and Saturday morning scrapple breakfasts.

My parents and I played board games on that table, and my friends and I played there too. It was the table where my father could smack me with a backhand if I upset him while we were eating. It was the table where, eventually, my own grandparents joined us when they moved into our house, when I was a young teenager. It was the table where Scott and I told my parents that we wanted to get married.

Then, years later, that table was in my mother's apartment, and it became the place where we looked at her funeral lists, and where we looked at the brochures for assisted living facilities, and finally, where we sat to sort through pages and pages of Maryland real estate listings. Now, it was a family table again, and my mother had the seat of honor, as she called it, at the head of the table. It was also the seat closest to the den, so she didn't have to walk too far to get to it.

Her seat faced the double glass doors leading out onto our deck, so she could look at the woods from this angle too. She loved staring at the view, and she was especially tickled because the folded blue umbrella in the middle of our deck table reminded her of Mary Poppins from the movie. The umbrella had a flap around the top part, and I guess it sort of resembled the little cape that went around the shoulders of Mary Poppins' coat.

When the umbrella was belted closed, as it was all winter long, that belt probably looked like a waistline. But it annoyed me that she kept calling our umbrella *Mary Poppins*, as in, "Oh, Mary Poppins has some snow on herself today," or, "Look at Mary Poppins blowing in the wind!" I'm not sure why it bothered me so much, but it really did. So, I'm ashamed to say that I don't think

I ever let on to her that I could see the resemblance too. I let her think she was the only one who saw it.

From the day we moved in, her breakfast was almost always toast with butter and jelly, orange juice, and coffee with cream and sugar. I tried to get her to vary it, but she really enjoyed that *jelly bread,* as she called it. The exception was weekend breakfast, when she'd have cereal, just like Scott was having, and the two of them would split a banana.

Every single Saturday and Sunday, they'd do their banana routine. He'd make a big production of peeling one, and she'd pretend that she was waiting patiently for her half, while making a show of raising her eyebrows to hurry him along.

She'd smile a cheesy grin, saying, "Oh, thank you, sir!" when he'd hand the banana half to her.

"My pleasure, my good lady!" he'd reply.

The joke never got old for them, but I'd roll my eyes and find something else to do while they did their weekend banana shtick. Honestly, I was glad they got along so well. Weekend meals were much easier for me because Scott was there to entertain her.

After realizing that her hands were shaking too much to hold her cups and mugs, and having her ask for straws every day, I searched online and ordered some plastic reusable mugs that had large, thick handles which were easy to grip, and lids with washable straws. I bought a set of four mugs, each a different bright color, but after seeing that she could go through all four by mid-day, including one for water and one for iced tea, I ordered more.

Again, she told me I was a genius for finding something so simple. On the few occasions that she went to respite care, I wrote her name in permanent marker on a few of those mugs so that she could take them along.

Her lunches varied a lot more than her breakfasts did. But there was a period when I made grilled cheese sandwiches for her every single day for two weeks. It really *was* similar to when my kids were little and fussy and wanted the same thing all the time. Once in a while, I could talk her into a ham and cheese or a tuna salad sandwich, but she often preferred *platters,* also similar to what I used to make for my daughters, with some slices of cheese, crackers, and grapes.

Occasionally, she'd accept apple slices, but it usually had to be red seedless grapes. She could put the plate on her side table and nibble as she watched TV shows.

I am fairly certain that Andy Griffith was in almost everything my mother watched on TV. Between her breakfast and lunch, and in the early afternoons, I'd try to work. I had to concentrate carefully on everything I did, because the TV had to be blaringly loud for her to enjoy *the programs*, as she called them. I'm surprised that my work emails didn't contain quotes from Barney Fife and Matlock, because their voices seemed to be inside my head constantly.

Although, in fairness, she did give equal time to watching some Catholic shows on EWTN, the Eternal Word Television Network. It was a real challenge for me to try to read work messages and compose reports and newsletters while hearing the meditative drone of a group of nuns saying the Rosary out loud for a half hour. I often felt like I was being lulled to sleep.

Some of the homilies spoken by the priests during the daily TV masses made me wish I could put in earplugs. But I needed to be able to hear my mother whenever she called for me, which was pretty often, so I had to learn to tune out the audio distractions.

The use of the TV also had to be carefully considered when we first moved in, because I knew that watching the news together had potential to be very uncomfortable. Our differing political views were a hurdle that threatened to be insurmountable at times. My mother and I had opposing views, and having her living with my family during a time when the political divide in our country seemed to overshadow everything else, well, it was rough.

My extended family had a history of letting politics come between us at times, and with the most recent presidential election, I had to drive my mother to an eye doctor appointment the morning after the votes were in. I'd been up very late, watching election results with disbelief and horror, as the candidate I preferred lost the election. I knew that driving with my mother the very next morning would be a challenge, so I braced myself and tried to steer our conversation to other subjects. But she couldn't resist, and she actually began to gloat.

She opened the topic by saying that she felt so relieved that her candidate had won. And yes, she knew that I was in favor of the other one. She went on to list her reasons for why this would be so much better for the country than if my candidate had won. I interrupted her and asked her to talk about something else. She said that she just wanted me to understand that this election result was such a positive thing.

I told her that I could not be convinced of that, but that I respected the election process, and I asked her to please stop talking about this. I actually told her that she was being a *poor winner*, a bad sport, about it. "Enjoy that your candidate won," I told her, "and please stop talking about this while I'm driving, because I'm very sad about this, especially today, the morning after the election."

But she was relentless and she continued to try to persuade me, with example after example, none of which seemed accurate to me, even though she was well aware that I'd been very active in my own political party for many elections prior.

It was crazy for her to think that she could change my mind, but she made some wild accusations about my candidate, and I lost it. I raised my voice and finally yelled at her, "Just be quiet!" I took a breath and followed up with, "If you can't stop talking about the election, then don't ask me to drive you to appointments any more. You're in *my* car, and I don't want to talk about this."

Even after that, she kept it up, and I kept angrily repeating, "I don't want to talk about this."

She reprimanded me as if I was a child, "How dare you raise your voice to your mother! I'm entitled to my opinion!" And I told her that I was also entitled to *my* opinion and that I didn't want to listen to her any more trying to persuade me that my opinion was wrong. When we got to the doctor's parking lot, my mother jumped out of my car faster than I'd ever seen her move. I hadn't even put the car into Park when she had her door open.

She had her walker with her, and she actually pulled the walker out of the car and opened it herself, which was very unusual. She was showing strength that I'd never seen in recent years, probably from adrenaline. She started walking away from my car so fast that I was afraid she'd step into traffic in the parking lot. I rushed around to her side of the car and closed her car door, which she'd left open, and ran after her.

I grabbed onto her walker just as she was about to step into the traffic lane, and I told her that she was going in the wrong direction. In her anger, she was heading away from the doctor's building.

"Please!" I begged her, "Just stop this and let me walk with you. Let's just stop talking about the election, and this will be fine." She didn't respond but she did let me lead her in the correct direction toward the right building. When we got to the waiting room, it was empty, so I apologized for raising my voice in the car. I said that I was sorry if I upset her, and that I knew I shouldn't have yelled at my mother.

This seemed to placate her, and she said, finally, "Well, I guess we don't have to talk about this."

When we knew that she'd be moving in with us, I gave a lot of thought to how we would manage political conversations. The only solution I could find, which was painful for me, was to avoid talking about politics at home completely. When I gave her the remote control for the TV and wrote out all the listings for different channels in large print, I omitted her favorite news source.

In fairness, I also vowed not to watch my own favorite news channel while she lived with us. I didn't see the need for either of us to torture the other. When we watched the news, which was rare, we stuck to local network news, which seemed fine to both of us. We sat together and watched the horrible fire at Notre Dame, because my mother wanted to watch that all day when it happened, but I don't really remember watching much more than local weather at other times.

I knew that watching news in our house would only create difficulty between us, so I had to silence my own sense of conviction. I felt like I was muzzled for months, but there were no political arguments while we lived together, and I believe that that was a huge accomplishment. A painful but huge accomplishment.

After a few weeks of our togetherness, I had the idea to put some jingle bells onto my mother's walker so that she could just shake it when she needed me. I figured that I would hear the bells more easily than her usually quiet voice, and it would also mean that she wouldn't have to strain to call out for me. Being a musical family, we had a lot of instruments, and I found a green wristband that resembled a bracelet full of bells.

It was probably left over from my days teaching preschool music, but it fit perfectly onto the handle of her walker. The added advantage of having the bells on the walker was that I could also hear her coming, which alleviated my fright from those first few weeks when I'd be typing away for work and glance up to see her peering around the corner, smiling and waving at me from the hallway. So often, I'd be startled and jump in my seat when I'd see her unexpectedly watching me. Scott said that she would have been great on a stealth mission.

We also became keenly aware that there was no such thing as a private conversation in our house. If my mother realized that we were in another room talking, she would almost always join us. Even when Zoe came home for spring break and we needed to talk with her about how things were going at college, including some matters that didn't require my mother's input or opinion, my mother would simply walk into the room with her walker and sit down with us.

She expected to be included in every conversation, even when we had clearly tried to separate ourselves to talk privately. At least the jingle bells gave us a heads-up when she was on the way.

But I knew that she liked conversation. In the late afternoons with my mother, I'd try to make sure that I had some time to sit with her in the den, and sometimes in the living room, but she was most comfortable in that old recliner. We'd sit side by side facing the TV, which was sometimes turned off so that we could talk. Sometimes, though, she'd want the TV left on and we'd try to talk over it.

If I was especially tired, I'd try to find an old movie, maybe a musical or a mystery, and we'd just sit together and watch. Her attention span was already getting much shorter and she'd usually fall asleep partway through. When that happened, I'd usually close my eyes too, or else I'd sneak away to get something done in another room.

Once in a while, I'd be able to talk her into watching something new, something that she hadn't seen before. Her favorite by far was *Newsies*, the Broadway musical, which was streaming on Disney+. It might have been the only time that she didn't fall asleep during a movie, although we did take a snack break at intermission. She actually sat forward while that show was on our TV, and she was mesmerized by the dancing newsboys.

Maybe it's because the Children's Crusade story was familiar to her, or maybe because she enjoyed the historical 1899 setting, but it thrilled her. She also raved about Jeremy Jordan, who had the leading role. She told me that his voice was like an angel, and I actually heard her sigh while he was singing the poignant and powerful song *Santa Fe*.

Afterward, I found a few more videos of Jeremy Jordan singing on YouTube, and I showed all of them to her. She said that he was very handsome, and when she found out that Zoe also adored him, she said that Zoe had very good taste. I was honestly kind of touched to see my mother, at age ninety-three, exhibit a little bit of a crush.

We did have some fun together, but most of the time, I would have rather been doing almost anything else other than sitting alone with her in the den. I was already feeling the drag of monotony as our days seemed repetitious with the same activities and the same kinds of conversation. On most days, I'd find myself counting down to Scott coming home from work, just because I was longing for another person to be in the house, especially one who understood me.

By dinnertime, I'd be tired and lonely, wishing for my own life back without the responsibility of caring for my mother's needs. But I'd have to prepare something for her dinner. She usually didn't want the same things that we were eating. I had planned to make home cooked meals for her much more often than I actually did, because her finicky tastes made it difficult. I tried quite a few recipes for things that I thought she would enjoy, but she'd wrinkle up her nose and make a face when I'd tell her what I was cooking.

She often requested things like chicken tenders with gravy, or mashed potatoes with gravy, or even Italian meatballs with gravy. Brown gravy was the common theme in most of her dinner requests, and she also really like prepared and frozen foods. When I'd offer her oven-roasted fresh veggies, she would say that they didn't taste anything like *real* vegetables. They needed some butter and salt, she'd tell me. She was not a fan of garlic or most other seasonings.

She did enjoy frozen green beans, with butter and salt, of course, and she loved my homemade macaroni and cheese. I tried to mix it up by making other things she might like, such as meatloaf or pasta, but she'd ask for brown gravy on both. But one very good thing about being in Maryland was that my mother loved crabcakes. She had always loved them, and we found that all the local markets offered crabcake fixings all the time.

So, crabcakes became a regular, frequent dinner at our house, and I'd make fresh corn and cut hers off the cob, and usually a salad and fries. My mother would still ask for gravy to put onto her fries. I'd sometimes notice her dipping the crabcake into the gravy too. No wonder she so often complained of stomach aches.

Occasionally, we'd order carry-out food for dinner, and we'd always ask my mother what she'd like. Usually, she'd say that she didn't want anything from a restaurant, and she'd ask for her usual frozen food options. Almost always, when our food would arrive, she'd look over at my plate and say, "Ooh! That looks good!" And then she'd want some of my dinner.

So, I quickly got in the habit of ordering something extra that I thought she'd like, even when she said she didn't want anything. Otherwise, if I didn't do that, I'd have to be prepared to surrender my own meal to her, and I'd wind up eating her chicken tenders.

Her absolute favorite thing each day was dessert. I remember that we usually had some sort of dessert after dinner when I was growing up, maybe pudding or Jell-O or a store-bought pie. But at our house, she got a bit spoiled, I think. Our local Wegmans had a variety of cakes and pies, and we started to pick up something that she would enjoy every time we went grocery shopping.

She'd excitedly ask every day, "What's for dessert?" and she'd crane her neck to see if we had something waiting on the kitchen counter. She'd wiggle her eyebrows in anticipation when I'd open the bakery boxes. Eventually, it got to the point that instead of asking what the dessert would be, she'd ask what the dessert *choices* were.

I remember Scott laughing and answering her, "Oh, just a moment, and I'll be by with the dessert cart!"

We also finished each day with what we called *Grandmom's Special Recipe*, which was something I'd mix up for her after dinner each evening, consisting of applesauce, cinnamon, sugar, and morphine. Just a few drops for that extra flavor. On its own, the morphine was too strong a taste for her, and she said that pudding was awful with the liquid morphine mixed in.

But the combination of applesauce with a heavy hand on the cinnamon and a bit of extra sweetness seemed to do the trick. My mother was a person who rarely took medicine during her lifetime. She didn't even like to take acetaminophen. She'd complain about pain often, but she wouldn't take anything to ease it. But the hospice nurse explained that the morphine was prescribed for her, in a very low dose, to help with her breathing.

Prior to taking the morphine, during those weeks right before we moved, she barely slept from being short of breath and feeling heaviness in her chest. The morphine relieved that pretty quickly, and she started sleeping without that breathing distress.

It was difficult to watch her declining, and although she was still clear-thinking and wanted to have control, I could see her slowing down. She leaned more heavily onto her walker, and the trips up the stairs became less frequent during the day, with her eventually only wanting to come down once in the morning and then only one more walk up the stairs to go back up in the evening. She no longer asked to go upstairs during the day.

As I'd walk her up the stairs each evening, with my hand on her lower back, I'd have to give her firm support and sometimes actually push her a little bit so that she could propel herself up to the next step. She'd hang onto the railing with both hands, gripping as tightly as she could, but I knew that if I ever stepped away, she'd go tumbling down backwards. I tried not to imagine that, and I always stayed very close behind her.

Only a caregiver knows how it feels to be always walking behind someone on stairs, as they struggle to lift themselves, one foot in front of the other, climbing and struggling, and the humbling position of having the person's bottom almost directly in your face. But you thank God that you still have the ability to be in the position of strength, and you keep going, helping them to get to the top.

During those slow climbs each evening, I'd often think of the song *Walk Him Up the Stairs* from the musical *Purlie*. I had sung that song twice with my choir, the Abington Choral Club in Glenside. I still knew the alto harmony and most of the lyrics, and sometimes I'd even hum it to myself as we went up together. The song is actually about a funeral, and the idea of walking someone up the stairs is a metaphor for going to Heaven.

The arrangement my choir sang started with a slow and soulful verse before it picked up the tempo and became a spirited jazzy piece that made people want to dance and clap. It was a joyful song, and the thought of it being appropriate for the end of life made me smile. We were certainly on a difficult climb, but I knew that there's also something beautiful about being present during someone's last days.

My choir first performed that song shortly after my father died, and it was bittersweet for me. And now, as I sang it quietly to myself, I felt that melancholy again.

The walks up the stairs also reminded me of my mother's own gracefulness when she cared for her own parents in our family home when I was a young teen. My sisters were both basically gone, one married and one in college, when my grandparents, Oma and Opa, moved into our house. Opa was very confused all the time by then, and Oma was very frail.

They moved into the bedroom that had been mine, which was closest to the bathroom, and I moved into the larger bedroom that my sisters had shared growing up. When my middle sister came home on breaks from college, we shared that room.

Oma and Opa would sit in our living room all day most days, watching game shows and reruns on TV. Oma would walk around and try to help with things, but she wasn't able to do much. We all shared one bathroom, although we had a half bathroom down in the basement. I started to use that a lot more after they moved in with us because Oma was very slow with her bathroom routine, and my mother had to help Opa with everything.

I remember watching my mother wash her father's feet in a basin, and every single evening, she'd walk him up the stairs. Our stairs in that house on Alcott Street were right in the living room, so I'd sit on the sofa and watch her. Opa was tall and muscular, and my mother had to support him on each step, just as I was doing now with her, although she was so much smaller than him. I don't remember her complaining, but I do remember her crying sometimes. Just quietly crying.

I'd sit with her and hug her, not fully understanding what it was like for her. Not fully understanding until now.

So, my mother's position had shifted. The *walker* became the *walkee*. And it seemed to me that walking up the stairs was becoming a richly symbolic full circle moment for my mother, as well as a rite of passage for me.

After each night's walk, we'd get her ready for bed. Her evening habits were slower than the morning ones, and I often felt tired and impatient. I'd help her into her nightgown, robe and bedtime socks, and then we'd go through her slow and methodical bathroom routine. Her hands were so shaky that I'd put the toothpaste onto her toothbrush, and I'd set her towels on the sink where she could easily reach them. She'd wash up and put moisturizer on her face.

Sometimes she could manage alone in the bathroom, and sometimes I'd have to stay to help her, before we'd head back into her overly warm bedroom, where the electric space heater was already blasting at full capacity. She loved the warmth, but it made me sweat, which didn't help my mood. I'd roll my eyes behind her back as she slowly double-checked that her water cup, her cough drops, her tissues and her rosary were all in place on her nightstand.

If her bed looked at all messy from having been sat on, she'd actually try to straighten the covers *before* she got in. I eventually got in the habit of making sure that the bed covers were smooth before bringing her upstairs, because it would save five full minutes of her painstakingly rubbing her hands across the blankets. When it looked okay, she would fold back the top corner of her sheets into an almost perfect triangle so that she could sit down on the uncovered space and prepare to get into bed.

That was when my agitation would really flair. She'd sit there, night after night, and come up with any number of things that needed to be discussed or resolved before she'd agree to swing her legs into the bed. Sometimes, if felt like torture to me. None of the subjects she'd bring up at bedtime were actually so important that they couldn't wait until the next day.

I'd have to stand there every night, listening to her concerns and waiting. It would be so close to me having my chance to go back downstairs for an hour or so of free time, but she'd delay.

Sometimes, she'd have a list tucked into the pocket of her robe, so I knew that it was probably something that she wrote out early in the morning and saved for the end of the day. Usually she was clarifying things that really didn't need her attention right then, like grocery lists or plans for the next few days. Often, she wanted to go over the schedule of the hospice workers' visits for the upcoming week, even though she'd never remember from one day to the next.

Sometimes, she wanted to tell me about her pain and stiffness, and those were the nights when I knew I was trapped, because how could I possibly walk away when she was uncomfortable. So, I'd rub cream on her back and gently massage her, or I'd rub cream on her feet. We used Aspercream, but she regularly called that cream *Mrs Meningitis*. I have no idea where she came up with that name, but she'd use it as if that was the common name for the product, as in, "It feels so good when you rub Mrs Meningitis on my feet."

Sometimes, she'd pat the bed next to her and she'd just want me to sit down for a while. We'd sit there side by side, and she'd thank me for taking care of her, and I'd begrudgingly tell her that I was glad to have her living with us. I understood, even in those moments, the value of that time together, and I'd try my best to appreciate it fully.

But I know that there were too many times when I had to swallow my desire to just get up and leave, from exhaustion and frustration. *Please, please let me go back downstairs, away from you for a few minutes.* Sometimes, I literally had to beg her to put her feet into the bed so that I could cover her, kiss her cheek, turn off her big light, and get out of there.

But no matter what else had happened during her bedtime preparation, I always left the room the same way. I'd back out of the doorway, leaving her with her nightlight and the hum of the space heater, and I'd wave my hand up and down, the same way she waved to me from her bed.

"Sleep tight," I'd say every night, as I slowly closed her bedroom door. I said the same little phrase every single night. "Sleep tight, Mommy. I love you!"

"Good night, my sweetheart," she'd reply. "I love you, too. You're my good friend."

Once in a while, if I had to drive to Pennsylvania for work, or when I desperately needed a break, Scott handled my mother's bedtime routine. He would walk her up the stairs and he has his own memories of rubbing cream on her back and helping her get tucked into her bed. He was gentle and kind with her, and she told him often that he was like a son to her.

She didn't seem to make him sit with her for the lengthy talks, as she did with me, but she seemed completely comfortable with him and they laughed together much more often than I laughed with her.

On one of the evenings when I was feeling especially energetic, I decided to take the opportunity to try to resolve some of my emotional pain with my mother, because I was realizing that time might be short. She was sitting on the side of her bed, as usual, and she started to talk about the night my father died. She was pondering, as she often did, about whether or not there was anything we could have done differently so that he wouldn't have died that night.

She was getting fuzzy on some of the details, so she asked me to once again walk her through everything that had happened on that night. I wanted, or rather *needed*, to talk with her about what she'd said to me in the hospital. I was hoping that maybe after ten years, she might have reconsidered that stance and might regret having said what she said. I even thought that maybe she'd apologize to me, which would feel so healing.

So, after we talked through what had happened at their house on the night he died, I asked her if she remembered what she'd said to me at the hospital. She didn't. So, I reminded her.

"Mom, you turned around to me, right after we went into the room with Daddy, and the first thing you said to me was that he'd wished he would have lived long enough to see me come back to church."

She paused. "I never said that."

"You did, and it really hurt me at the time."

"I don't remember saying that," she replied. Another pause. I could see that she was thinking about it.

"But actually, if I *did* say something like that, it was because it was true."

Oh, no.

"Your father wanted more than anything for you to come back to church. His dying wish was that you'd remember that you're Catholic and rejoin our Faith. And he died before that happened."

This was worse than I could have imagined. It felt like another punch. Not only was she reinforcing the same sentiment, she was again saying that I'd disappointed my father, as well as her, and also implying that I might *still* go back to being Catholic someday. It was my own fault this time. I shouldn't have brought it up. I should have known better.

This time, though, I told her a little bit about my spiritual journey and how my new faith community felt like a better fit for me. I told her that I respected her faith but that I didn't feel the same way.

"Well, those Quakers are very nice people," she said. "Your Granny, that's Daddy's mother," (as if I didn't know that) "she worked for a Quaker man when she worked at Stetson Hat Company. He was very good to her, and she respected him a lot." I guess it was her way of telling me that I could have done worse.

But I felt the tears coming, so I told her that I needed to get to bed myself and helped her to put her feet into her own bed. I needed to leave before the room closed in on me. My 'Sleep tight', was a bit briefer that night, and as I walked away from her bedroom, I reminded myself that she was still trying to save my soul. I had to keep telling myself that.

A few days later, when we were once again reviewing her funeral program, she told me that if we couldn't find a good restaurant for the funeral luncheon, maybe I could find out if we could use the social room at the Quaker meetinghouse where I worked. I was amazed. I told her that I'd need to ask for permission when the time came, but we started to talk more about the meetinghouse, which she had visited once several years earlier, when I had her in the car with me as I was dropping something off at work.

At that time, she was very interested in the beautiful grounds and the historical building. I had walked her through and she admired it.

"We could have the luncheon in that big room, and maybe you could get a caterer," she offered, and I knew that this was the biggest olive branch ever. She was giving me consent.

"I liked that room," she went on, "with the beautiful grand piano."

I told her about the history of that piano, and to my astonishment, we realized that the man who donated the piano to the meetinghouse many years earlier had been a friend of my Opa. My mother remembered her father talking about that man and they'd played German music together. That relation was confirmation for me that everything truly was connected in our world. And I felt my beloved grandfather's presence in the conversation.

In the end, we used a restaurant for her funeral luncheon, because it was simply easier, but I never forgot that she made that overture about gathering at the meetinghouse for her own send-off. It was a step toward the healing that I needed.

My mother's sense of humor never wavered, even when she was getting a bit more confused. Sometimes, she was hilariously funny without intending to be. I remember one spring day when Zoe and I were sitting on our deck with my mother, and we were listing to the many birds chirping and making a variety of sounds in the trees nearby.

We knew that my mother loved birds, and she even once identified an Oriole immediately when it landed on our deck railing. So, Zoe asked her if she was able to identify different birds from their sounds. My mother got excited, and she assured Zoe and me that she could definitely do this. She started to demonstrate her bird call knowledge by making the sounds for us.

She sat there in the white plastic rocking chair, trying her very best to whistle, but the sounds coming out were feeble and barely audible. But she didn't seem to realize that we could hardly hear her. We just sat there watching her, with her puckered lips, as she seemed to be doing bird calls that only she could hear. And then she suddenly said, quite triumphantly, "There! That's what the different birds sound like!"

Zoe and I couldn't help ourselves but laughed pretty hard. My mother laughed too, obviously thinking that our laughter came from us being so impressed by what she could do.

We'd also had a wonderful evening when we sat around the table after dinner one night. We had some music playing on the stereo in the next room, and my mother started drumming on the table. It started with her using her spoon to clink her empty iced tea glass, and then she added raps on her dinner plate. She then used her left hand to start to press her Snapple lid to make a popping sound, and she alternated the pattern and added more sounds, all done in perfect time to the music that was playing.

I felt like we were watching a toned down version of *Stomp*, with my mother using ordinary objects as rhythm instruments. And her facial expressions added the comical element, as if she surprised herself with every new sound she made. Zoe couldn't stop laughing, and Scott joined in, tapping his knife too.

I started to write down some of my mother's funniest quotes, just because I knew that I'd want to remember. She had always been quick to laugh at herself, so I knew that on some level she'd appreciate that we were laughing with her. Her comments were becoming more and more bizarre.

One day, out of nowhere, she said, "Tarzan, that poor soul. Maybe he's a leprechaun and that's why he yodels!" She liked to refer to people as *poor souls*.

Another day, when we'd all been sitting quietly in the living room, and no one had spoken for a few minutes, and my mother said, "That's a good question."

She used to joke that she wanted to live in our shed out back, because it would be her own little house. I'd remind her that there was no bathroom or heat, and then she'd say in mock disappointment, "Oh, well, then I'd better stay here in the house."

Scott was talking about his job one evening, and my mother said, "That's very interesting. And boring." Scott burst out laughing and acknowledged that she was actually correct.

And there was the time we watched the old musical *Seven Brides for Seven Brothers*. As the movie was concluding, my mother said, "That Howard Keel is a marvelous singer."

I asked, "Wasn't he in *Showboat* too?"

"No," she replied, "that was Howard Keel."

I also remember the time that Scott was talking about his teenage years, and he mentioned his selective service registration. "If I hadn't been a college student," he said, "I might have gotten drafted."

I responded, "Yeah, and I guess you would have gone to Vietnam."

And my mother chimed in, "Or Anchorage."

But her geography confusion didn't end there. One Saturday morning, we were sitting at the kitchen table and the conversation went like this:

Scott: "What was the 48th state, before Alaska and Hawaii?"

Me: (Looking it up on my phone) "Go ahead and guess."

Scott: "New Mexico. Washington. California."

My mother: "Ontario."

Scott: (Trying not to laugh) "Florida. Arizona."

My mother: "Jamaica."

But sometimes her quirky phrases and comments weren't so amusing. She could dig in with her concerns and drive me crazy. I remember a warm, sunny day in the spring when I said, "It's a beautiful day! I'm going to open some windows." She became very alarmed at the idea of open windows.

"Do you have screens?" she asked, with great concern.

"Yes," I replied. "All of the windows have screens."

She persisted, "Does the screen cover the whole window?"

"Yes, all the windows have full screens."

"I'm not sure that they do," she started to get more agitated. "You better not open the windows."

"Mom, it's okay," I continued. "We just need some fresh air in here."

"*You* may need fresh air, but I'm fine without it."

As I went around opening the windows, I heard the jingle bells on her walker as she followed me from room to room, shaking her head and making 'tsk, tsk' noises behind me, expressing her disapproval and annoyance. When the windows were open, she asked me every few minutes how long it would be until I closed them again. I think I caved in after about an hour and just closed them. The warm breezes weren't strong enough to blow away my frustration.

Another time, I regretted having the windows open again, but for a different reason. I had contacted a local nursing home to ask if they knew of a hair stylist who made house calls. My mother desperately wanted her hair cut because it was getting long, by her standards. I made arrangements for the hair stylist to come to our home and as the female hair stylist walked toward our house from her car, my mother looked out the open window from the den and started to yell to me, "That's not the hairdresser! It's a man!"

I quickly came into the den to calm her. "Shh! It is a woman," I said. "She just has short hair." This wasn't an issue of gender identity; it was an issue of my mother thinking that women should not have hair that short.

But my mother was adamant. "That's a man!" She hollered, and I'm sure the stylist heard her, and politely ignored her and, thankfully, kept walking to our door to ring the bell. "That looks just like a man," my mother persisted, "and you said it would be a woman!"

I hardly knew what to do and I felt my face reddening as I opened the door. But the hair stylist was kind, and as soon as she stepped inside, my mother had a complete turn-around and welcomed her warmly. The whole thing made me want to cry. But at least she got a beautiful hairdo, and we sent photos to my sisters of my mother posing with the stylist.

My mother was like that with anyone who came into the house. No matter how upset she'd been before their arrival, she was pleasant and friendly when someone came in. We had a contractor working on a few things inside and outside, and my mother was very upset by the noise, but when he spoke to me, and my mother heard his Irish accent, she called out to him from the other room, "What part of Ireland are you from?"

He graciously stepped into the den to greet her and he told her a bit about his family's county in Ireland, and my mother showed all of her Irish-wannabe personality. My father had been of Irish descent, but my mother's ancestors were one hundred percent from Germany. But when she married my father, she became an honorary Irish woman, and she seemed to be more interested in Irish culture and history than my father was.

This came through clearly as she spoke with the contractor, and he even asked me if I minded if he sat down for a few minutes to talk with her. Of course, I didn't mind. She enchanted him with her own stories about trips to the Emerald Isle, and he seemed to enjoy the conversation. I even brought them both some iced tea while they visited.

Around that same time, my mother also had a volunteer from the hospice start to visit occasionally. Like all hospice volunteers, myself included (because I had become a volunteer after concluding my hospice employment), she was trained in aspects of the hospice mission and protocols. She came to visit three times, always in the evening for an hour or two, just to sit and talk with my mother so that Scott and I could both go out together.

Twice, he and I went to a local restaurant to have a quick bite and to enjoy some time without the constant presence of my mother. We had to try hard not to spend our precious alone-time talking about her. The other time, we used the volunteer's visit to attend our Homeowners Association meeting and finally meet some neighbors.

Each time, when we came home, my mother and her friendly visitor would be talking about culture and customs. The volunteer was born in India, and again, my mother was fascinated by her stories and about world cultures.

Still, the days went by slowly. I had no idea how long my mother would be with us, and the vision I had of her lingering for years wasn't always a happy one. I was noticing that I was losing my sense of self because I was constantly distracted by my mother's comments, my mother's needs, my mother's preferences.

Looking out the windows became something very different for me. I'd look out across the street and imagine the people in those houses doing exactly what they wanted to do all the time. I'd look out but I'd be listening to her talking just behind me. Or I'd look out the window by the sink while washing dishes and I'd wonder what it would feel like to be outside right at that moment, instead of inside, in this house, with my mother constantly nearby. I felt trapped, and I felt guilty for feeling trapped.

I was acutely aware that my thoughts and feelings might get worse, because there was no relief in sight, no end-date, no sense of what the future would hold. The present reality seemed like it could continue indefinitely, and that was possibly more than I could handle.

Breakdown

If I lose my mind,
will I notice?
Or will I just slide
into a happy oblivion,
unaware of the adjustment,
blind to the new worldview?
Maybe I could tell a friend
to let me know
if I become someone else
something else
no longer the me
people recognize.
Maybe it will be like a game
of chutes and ladders
when I'm approaching the winning square and suddenly
shoot downwards
back to a place before the journey began.
Or maybe I'll be like Bill Murray waking up
to the same day over and over, or different days
out of order, or
an eternal spin cycle
shuffling the memories,
mixing the experiences.
And I'll never know
what should be known.
A poetic conclusion
to the confusion of Life.

Chapter 6
The Beginning of the End

My mother: "I'm telling you, those seedless grapes are not seedless!"
Scott: "Did you get a seed in one of yours?"
My mother: "No."

My husband, Scott, and my mother, Ellen, age 93

Leaving the Catholic Church was probably the most difficult thing I've ever done. I did it because I needed to be true to myself. I had grown up being taught and believing that I could find all the answers I needed in Catholicism, but I eventually discovered that the questions themselves mattered more to me than the answers. I embraced the questions of life, and I came to enjoy being a seeker, a person searching and always learning.

I knew that Catholicism works for many people, but it wasn't the right path for me. I did not make my choice lightly and I wrestled with all of the complicated aspects of what my choice would mean both for myself and for my family. But as I made my choice, I came to peace with my spiritual path. I knew I had done the right thing for myself, and that I had acted with integrity.

But suddenly, I found myself facing my mother daily, all day every day, with her prayer books and her rosary beads, and her Catholic TV shows blaring in my own home. And I felt the full weight of disappointing my mother.

Never in my whole life did I doubt that she loved me, but I knew with certainty that I disappointed her. Here I was, living with this beautiful and sweet woman, this woman who had given me everything in life, and actually, given me life itself, but I was constantly aware that she wanted something else from me. And I could not give her that. Not even as her dying wish.

And she was definitely dying, although I didn't fully realize that until the very end.

We started to notice that she was declining at a more rapid pace in the middle of the spring. During the first few months with us, she appeared to have gained some weight, because her face filled out a bit and she seemed to look a bit less frail. We knew that it was likely happening because she was eating full meals regularly, and also because the morphine was helping her to breathe easier and sleep better.

Back in her apartment, she had probably been starting to skip meals or eating only things that were easy and quick to grab, because it was becoming difficult for her to manage. She eventually confessed that she also hadn't been sleeping before we moved, but I hadn't known that at the time. She had told us that she was getting along just fine, before her illness began.

My mother had always been a woman who was concerned about her weight, and even at her final in-office doctor appointment before we moved to Maryland, she was quite proud that the doctor told her that she'd lost five pounds since her previous visit. She didn't realize that he wasn't complimenting her. He was worried about her, but she talked about her 'weight loss' on the way home in my car, saying that she was so glad that she had lost some more weight.

She told me that she was just about where she wanted to be with her weight, as if she was on a self-improvement diet at age ninety-three. She was a small woman at that point, so deliberate weight loss seemed ridiculous to me.

Throughout her adulthood, she was quite sensitive about her size and weight, although I don't remember her ever seeming to look overweight. She even spoke with the hospice nurse about wanting to lose weight around her tummy. The hospice nurse just smiled and told her not to worry about it. The nurse was also amused, and somewhat alarmed, by my mother's pride of appearance when she'd asked my mother about a cut on her leg, and my mother replied that she'd cut herself while shaving her legs.

I had no idea that my mother was continuing to do that, so she must have been shaving her legs in the early mornings when she was alone in her bedroom, using her electric razor. I imagined that while holding it in her shaky hand, she must have bumped it into her leg hard enough to cause the cut on her shin. The hospice nurse advised her to stop shaving her legs, and my mother agreed, reluctantly.

Of course, when my mother had spoken so happily about her weight loss after that doctor appointment, I couldn't help but think of all those years I'd listened to her talk about losing weight. I had an obvious life-long problem with my own weight, but I was supposed to be happy for her. I was supposed to congratulate her on something that she didn't even understand to be a health concern.

I was supposed to tell my elderly mother that it was terrific that she was at her goal weight, probably due to her newly diagnosed heart disease, as I was sitting behind the steering wheel knowing that I was far above the ideal weight for myself. We drove along, with me sitting in silence, as she spoke about all her recent efforts to eat less.

When I reflected back on it later, thinking about all the times over the years when she seemed horribly insensitive to my weight struggle, I wondered if maybe it had been her passive aggressive way of reminding me to take care of my own weight. Maybe she wanted to invite me into a conversation about weight control, but I never took the bait. I understood my own crazy and unhealthy relationship with food, and I knew that hearing about it from her would only make me more resentful.

I wished she would have talked to me about it when I was a child or a teenager, when healthy food limitations might have set me on a different path. But it wasn't until after college that I learned, on my own, what I needed to do to control my weight, and I claimed responsibility for my size. The ups and downs since then were all on me, literally. My weight as an adult was not something that I wanted to discuss with her.

So, when she started to fill out a little bit in those early months with us, I didn't mention it to her. I didn't want her to think that I was a bad influence, although she was the one constantly asking for gravy and desserts. And that healthier, filled-out appearance didn't last too long anyway, despite the gravy. She started to lose more weight, which we could tell just by looking at her, and she also began to look more tired and sometimes pale.

Still, there were mornings when I'd go into her bedroom to find her twisting her pink and green plastic curlers into her hair. She'd be sitting on her bed with the dresser drawer where she kept her hair supplies open like a work-table in front of her. Sometimes, it would look as though she had wet her hair a little bit, probably using the leftover water from the cup on her nightstand. I imagine that she'd dipped her comb into that cup and then pulled it through her hair, just so that the curlers could take hold and do their work on the moistened hair.

I'd walk in to find her with the curlers and I'd have to quickly busy myself with restacking her folded clothes or straightening the curtains, just to avoid laughing. It was adorable, amusing, and a little bit sad all at the same time. Her appearance really mattered to her and she was trying to control whatever she could about how she presented herself. The curlers made her feel good.

I especially enjoyed walking with her into the kitchen on weekend mornings, when Scott would be at home, on curler days. The first time, he just stared at her for a moment before collecting himself and pulling out her chair for her at the table. He didn't know whether or not to acknowledge the curlers, but he wisely chose to keep quiet about them.

Subsequent curler days were no different, and he'd always give me a comical glare afterward, letting me know that he didn't appreciate my lack of a heads-up. He would have liked to prepare himself. Well, I would have liked that for myself too, but I figured that mornings like these gave me just enough humor to carry on with daily life.

As my mother started to seem weaker, she also started to seem more confused at times. At dinner one evening, she asked for more of 'those little tubes' meaning green beans. After that, she never knew the name of them again, her favorite vegetable. She'd struggle to describe them, but she just seemed to have lost those words. It happened just like that, with her suddenly not being able to recall the words *green beans* anymore.

She also became very confused in conversations with Scott about high school. As a young girl, my mother had attended Philadelphia High School for Girls, and Scott, many years later, attended Central High School, which was for boys. Those schools were partnered, so we definitely saw the connection, but my mother started to lose track of Scott's age and her own age in relation to each other.

She lost sight of the individual schools too. She asked him fairly frequently if he'd had the same teachers that she'd had, or if he was in her classes at Girls High. At first, we laughed together because she was aging Scott up quite a bit, but then it became troubling, because she simply couldn't keep the ideas straight.

Sometimes, she would say things that were close to correct but just slightly off. It was amazing to see how her mind was working. It was like solving a puzzle as we tried to piece together what she meant. One afternoon, she walked past the front window and saw my car parked out front in our driveway as usual, and she remarked, seeming surprised, "Oh, your car is parked out front today. So, I guess Scott took your car to work instead of his own. Because your car is out front. Scott must have it."

She also started to mix up names. Occasionally, she referred to Scott as Fox, as in, "When will Fox be home?" At least Fox was his last name, so that wasn't quite as bad as some of the other names she called him. She sometimes called him Spot, which really made us chuckle. I told him he was a good boy. But my favorite of my mother's name mix-ups was the day that she referred to Scott as Start. It was like being in a *Who's on First* routine.

"Loretta, can you come here, and Start."

"Start what?"

"Bring him."

"Who?"

"Start."

"What do you want me to start?"

"Just bring him with you."

"Who?"

"Bring Start."

'*What?*' Pausing to think. "Oh…He's upstairs."

She asked me one day, "Would it be appropriate for me to call you Mrs Fox Black?" I told her it would not be appropriate because that's not my name. Where did the *Black* come from? And what was up with calling me *Mrs* anything? She had plenty of embarrassing, childish nicknames for me, when she didn't want to call me *Loretta*, including Shnookie, and Honeybunch, and Let-Let. There was no reason at all to call me Mrs, and especially not Mrs Something-Not-My-Name.

It made me laugh, but after I thought about it, I wondered if she was somehow connecting me to the actress Shirley Temple, whose name in adulthood was Shirley Temple Black. Maybe my mother was confusing me, her own *little girl*, with the former child star. I had no idea really, but I just wanted desperately for my mother's thought patterns to have meaning.

But even as she was declining, she was able to play the piano beautifully. Maybe it was muscle memory in her arthritic fingers, or maybe music had a special power over her, but I'd help her into the living room where she'd sit on the piano stool with her walker right behind her, delicately stroking the ebony and ivory keys on her upright piano, which was now part of our living room. She'd smile and quietly page through a book of folk songs, and then she'd begin to play.

Danny Boy was her favorite song, and she played that every time she sat at the piano. She also played folk dances and beautiful pieces that I'd heard so many times throughout my life. She said that she no longer had the coordination needed to play more complicated classical pieces, but it all sounded wonderful to me. I'm glad that I thought to video-record her playing piano, sitting there in her fleece robe, looking so proud of herself that she actually nodded to me at the end with a little bow.

Scott would say, "You know, sometimes your mother is really cute!"

She would also be so happy when Zoe would be home with us from college, because Zoe would play that piano and sing, and my mother absolutely loved listening. Zoe played show tunes and pop songs, and after every one, my mother would ask her if she wrote the song. My mother was just so pleased to see and hear her granddaughter playing and singing at that beautiful old piano, and Zoe enjoyed the enthusiastic audience my mother provided.

We continued to go on car rides, just to get out of the house, but it was becoming significantly more difficult to walk my mother to the car. On our few front steps, I basically had to lift her from one step to the next because she just couldn't manage. And we wouldn't be able to drive for too long before she'd say that she was tired.

We made the best of our days, but I was exhausted all the time.

Around that same time, Zoe sent me a beautiful floral arrangement to let me know that she was thinking of me. She was away at college at the time but she knew that I was struggling with taking care of her grandmother. So, she sent the cheery yellow and white flowers to remind me that this would all be okay.

When the flowers were delivered, I took them into the kitchen to unwrap them and cried a little as I read Zoe's thoughtful note to me. I carried the arrangement into the den to show my mother, and as I started to say that Zoe sent them to me, she interrupted, because she was so excited to see the flowers.

"Oh, I'll have to thank her!" she said. "That was so sweet of her to send me flowers! Can you help me call her? I can't believe that she sent those to me for no reason, but just because she wanted to make me feel good!"

I didn't have the heart to tell my mother that the flowers weren't for her. So, I placed a call to Zoe from the kitchen and I quickly whispered my own heartfelt thanks and explained her grandmother's confusion before handing the phone to my mother. Zoe played along nicely and laughed about the confusion.

But things were getting harder on so many levels. One afternoon while I was working at the dining room table, I heard a strange sound from the den. It sounded like paper being torn, and then I also heard my mother groaning. I rushed to the den to find her sitting forward in her recliner with an angry look on her face, tearing all the pages out of a book. Her hands were shaking but she was gripping the book with as much strength as she could muster, ripping handfuls of pages out.

"What are you doing?" I asked, completely startled to find her this way.

"This book!" she replied, through gritted teeth. "It doesn't make any sense, and the story is awful and full of nonsense!"

She continued her vengeful ripping of pages as I stepped closer and saw that it was one of her beloved German books, which she kept on a special shelf near her chair. These were books that she'd treasured for as long as I could remember, antique books that were written in German, which was her first language as a child. She had preserved these books over the years, and she had loved them.

I knew that it was too late for the book in her hand, as she was even pulling apart the binding with a force that shocked me. I felt myself starting to tremble because her behavior was so alarming and out of character. I got a bag for the paper that was all over the floor, and I decided not to argue with her. I cleaned up the mess and put on the TV right away, searching for one of her comedy favorites.

I brought her a new snack and I adjusted the drapes, hoping that maybe she'd fall asleep watching TV and feel better after a nap. That's exactly what happened. While she was sleeping, I thought about relocating some of her old books to a higher shelf, but I also knew that she was entitled to reach them when she wanted them. So, I left them where they were, and after that nap, she never mentioned the book-tearing again. I believe that, while sleeping, she forgot what she'd done.

I did speak with her hospice nurse, though, because the behavior was so upsetting. And I had to be honest in telling the nurse that it wasn't the only time that my mother had acted hostile in recent weeks. She had often reprimanded me, quite strongly, when I'd say or do anything that might disagree with what she had in mind. Even when I'd ask her if she was ready for dinner, she'd sometimes say that I was being bossy and mean.

Scott was fully aware of it too. We both had known that my mother had always had a tendency to do and say things that made her a bit difficult to be around at times. But this behavior and attitude seemed different and intensified.

There were also a few nights when I'd see the light under my mother's bedroom door or hear her moving around in her room in the middle of the night, and I'd go in to find her hard at work with projects that didn't seem logical at all. Once, she had most of her clothes from her closet piled on her bed in a heap, and she said that she was looking for some new outfits.

Another time, she had emptied her dresser drawers onto the bed and floor, so that she had piles of random things, papers and lists, hair accessories, handkerchiefs, socks, all scattered around her. Each time things like this happened, I'd have to clean everything up as quickly as possible for her to have room to get back into bed, but she'd berate me the whole time I was cleaning up, saying that I wasn't putting things away correctly and saying that I was *taking over*.

She also started to cry frequently. She'd cry at bedtime, and she'd cry first thing in the morning. I wasn't always clear on what was making her cry, but I wanted to fix it. I talked with the nurse and she started my mother on a low dose of medication for anxiety, which seemed to help. The medication also helped her to sleep a bit better at night.

But things continued to change, and I wasn't sure how much more I'd be able to handle. I shared my fear with the nurse. I was desperately trying to avoid placing my mother into the in-patient hospice care, which was like a nursing home, but I didn't really know how to do all of the things that my mother was starting to need. I probably would have placed her into nursing care if it hadn't been for the memory I had of my mother frequently saying that her worst fear was that she'd someday be in a nursing home.

She talked about it regarding her own parents, and talked about it for herself. She hated nursing homes, and I couldn't shake that memory of her begging me never to put her into one.

At one point, the nurse had asked me 'to take a look' every time my mother had a bowel movement. The nurse didn't trust that my mother was accurately describing her bowel habits, and there was some concern. But beside the fact that I simply didn't think I could do that every day, I also knew that my mother would hate having me do that as well. Still, I didn't want to shirk a task that needed to be done.

I was the caregiver after all. But after doing this requested check just once, my mother made it clear that we would not be continuing with it, and that was A-Okay with me. My mother was a smart woman, and even amid her decline, she had a lot of dignity. She knew the boundaries as well as I did. Still, my doubts about my continued capabilities were becoming more frequent, and I was afraid that I wouldn't be able to keep the promise that I'd made to my father about taking care of her.

The hospice social worker suggested that we try using occasional respite care for my mother. The Stella Maris facility offered short-term stays for all of the hospice patients in their care, and they encouraged the caregivers to use that option and get a break periodically to avoid burnout. I was hesitant because I knew that my mother would feel like she was being sent away.

I also knew that Scott and I wanted to go to New York City in May to see Abby walk with her graduating class from college, even though she'd actually finished back in December. The ceremony was important, and she'd be receiving her degree at Radio City Music Hall, and we didn't want to miss that. So, I agreed to use respite care so that we could leave my mother at the hospice while we attended that event, and the social worker also convinced me to let my mother try it out in advance too.

Because there was a two-night minimum for respite visits, I arranged a weekend respite for my mother. I talked with her about it, and the social worker talked with her about it, and even the chaplain talked with her and agreed to plan a visit while my mother was there. But the stress leading up to that respite weekend almost undid any relief that would come from the visit itself. My mother was in a complete panic about what it would be like and what she should take along.

She made three different lists of things to take, each list duplicating the others. I tried to reassure her that the hospice had given me very clear and complete instructions about what was needed, and that many patients did this all the time. It would be okay, I told her over and over. I guess she also didn't really understand why we would need a break, so the whole idea of going to respite care was inherently upsetting for her. She thought it was unnecessary.

Once she got there, though, it wasn't so bad. The respite wing in the hospice facility was lovely, with armchairs and a library and windows overlooking a reservoir. On the day I took her there, a nun came to visit her before I even left, which gave me great hope that this would go well. My mother was delighted to have the Sister of Mercy visiting, and she soon learned that the daily mass would be broadcast right into her room each day, and that someone would take her downstairs to the chapel, if she wanted.

My mother's volunteer also scheduled a visit for that weekend, so I felt confident when I finally walked out of the building about two hours after taking her there. She was well-settled and she knew that my sisters and I would all call her a few times a day.

The first respite weekend went very well, and my mother surprised me by saying that she'd be glad to go back during Abby's graduation ceremony weekend. That second respite visit was three nights, and it happened just a month later. Again, my mother was glad to be in a Catholic facility, and she seemed to trust that her care would be done well. My eldest sister even visited her at the hospice facility during that respite, and my mother was thrilled about that. But I knew that it wasn't easy for my mother to be away from us.

By the time I picked her up a few days later, with Abby along, my mother was ready to come home. During the car ride back to our house, she told us that a priest came to visit, and that the food was much improved since her first visit. I told my mother that maybe we could use respite care once in a while, or every few weeks, as the hospice recommended, so that I could get a rest from caregiving, but my mother got very upset.

I realized immediately that I should have waited to bring that up. I should have given her time to get home and recover her balance before suggesting that maybe she'd go back again. But I wanted to be clear that I needed a break sometimes. So, I held my ground and emphasized that she should be prepared to go back once in a while.

I felt mean, even as the words were leaving my mouth, because I could see how dejected she looked. She only wanted to be at home with us, but I stood firm. Sadly, that argument was completely unnecessary, because my mother never went back to respite care again. She would die just a few weeks later.

My mother also fell twice while she was in my care, and I had a very difficult time forgiving myself. It wasn't until much later when a friend who is a doctor told me that falls are expected with hospice patients, and that my presence probably prevented even more falls, that I felt a little better. But I know that I was at least partially responsible for the first fall.

It happened while Zoe was home for spring break. She was upstairs and Scott was in our basement working out, and I was starting to cook dinner. My mother had been sitting in her recliner in the den looking at a magazine. I put on some music on my phone, and decided to listen to my favorite Joni Mitchell songs as I was standing at the stove.

Maybe it was because Zoe was home and I was feeling especially lighthearted, or maybe I was having a few moments of forgetting that I was a caregiver, but I started to sing along. I was singing quietly because I actually didn't want anyone to hear me, but I was enjoying that moment by myself in the kitchen.

Then, I heard the jingle bells. I turned my head slightly and my mother was standing in the doorway with her walker and a huge grin, looking as if she was delighted to hear me singing, and to be honest, I knew that she always loved it when I sang for her. But I had wanted this moment to myself, and I rolled my eyes and stopped singing, and turned back to face my pan on the stove. It wasn't more than a minute later that I heard the crash in the den.

I spun around and saw that her walker was still in the doorway, but my mother wasn't there. I ran to the den and she was lying face up on the floor between the two chairs, and the small wooden table that usually stood in that spot was broken and splintered beneath her. I knew instantly that my reaction to her presence in the kitchen caused her to turn quickly and walk away, forgetting her walker in her rush. She probably lost her balance and reached out to lean on the table and fell onto it.

I yelled for Scott and Zoe to come help me, and I was able to stay calm and reassure my mother that she'd be okay. She was talking and she was embarrassed, so I guessed that the injury wasn't life threatening, not at that point anyway. She was trying to sit up on her own, but not quite able to manage it, and she said that the only thing that hurt was the back of her head.

I could see a lump already forming, and the back of her head was scraped and bleeding. Using the skills I'd learned while working in hospice, I knew how to lift her from the floor. I quickly gave Scott the instructions about what to do, and with one of us on each side, we looped our arms under her armpits, braced her feet from sliding forward, and gently lifted her into a chair. Zoe ran to get ice and Scott phoned the hospice. A nurse came by a short time later to look at my mother's head, and she told us that it wasn't serious, mostly just painful.

We gave my mother acetaminophen, because that was all she'd agree to take, and I also hoped that her evening serving of applesauce with cinnamon and morphine might help. My mother said that she was more humiliated than anything else. She thanked me for helping her and praised me for knowing how to lift her off the floor, but I knew that I didn't deserve that praise, because my eye rolling started the whole thing. Yes, she left her walker behind, which was happening more and more frequently, but I'd upset her enough to make her want to run away.

The second fall wasn't my fault, but she once again stood up and started walking without her walker. In fact, she had pushed it aside. This was about a month after the first fall. I had been working at my usual spot in the dining room while she was watching TV, when I heard the crash. I recognized the sound instantly and knew she'd fallen again.

I ran through the kitchen yelling, "I'm coming!" but I didn't hear a reply. I felt like my legs couldn't go fast enough. When I turned the corner into the den, she was on the floor, again face up, but with her head just inches away from the brick hearth of our fireplace. She was quiet but she was talking in a whispery way. I was alone in the house this time, so I tried by myself to calm her and check to see if anything seemed amiss.

She started to talk a bit more and I thought that she had probably been shocked by the fall, but seemed mainly okay. I checked her head and there were no signs that she'd bumped it again, and she was moving her arms and legs and trying to roll over. So, I used the familiar body mechanics to once again safely lift her up into a chair by myself. Her walker was pushed up against the bookshelf, where she'd obviously shoved it aside.

I called the nurse, and she came for a visit a short time later. She said that my mother was okay, but that she had a few bruises. Luckily, she'd fallen onto carpet and missed hitting any furniture this time. Even though I knew I couldn't have prevented this fall, I felt like my care was somehow lacking, because I should have known that she wanted to get up. But she didn't call me or ring her bells, so there was nothing I could have done differently. I just felt awful. Again.

There were days when my mother seemed so frail that I thought she wasn't going to survive another day. Some days, she didn't want to get out of bed, so she'd stay in her room all day. A few times, the nurse visited and told me to be prepared for anything. But then my mother's vital signs would improve and she'd be much better the following day. It was gut-wrenching to watch this, never knowing what was coming next.

I was feeling less and less sure of myself, and I wrote a long letter to myself one evening during those days, trying to capture and preserve how I felt at that moment. I suspected that I'd want to remember it. I needed to vent and writing has always been my way to get my thoughts out, to find clarity. I wanted to write out all my emotions so that I could reread it and get a clearer vision of how to move forward, and I think the writing helped me.

The phrase mixed emotions doesn't even begin to cover how I'm feeling right now. My mother declines and bounces back, one day on death's doorstep and the next day back in action. It happened twice this weekend. And today she's sitting here commenting on everything she sees out the window and everything she hears or sees inside our home. I feel like a horrible person being so angry all the time.

She has become the center of everything in this house, and I have no privacy and no time to myself. She calls for me all the time, like a toddler. Before we moved, I had anxiety attacks thinking about living with her, and it's exactly as I imagined, except that I didn't think she'd be so dependent so quickly. But today the aide said that my mom could still have many months left, and I felt myself get disappointed. I don't even like to admit that. I feel like an awful person.

I have been so privileged for all of my life. I have a beautiful family and home, and my daughters are thriving. I have Scott who loves me unconditionally and is the world's greatest friend. I love my job, really love it. And I've had two parents who loved me and cared for me growing up. At one time in my life, my mother was my best friend, and she was everything to me.

I've always had a home, enough food, and opportunities for education and work. Deep in my heart, I know that this present situation, which seems so small compared to all that I've been given, is meant to be an exercise in patience for me. I feel that it's meant to be a test for me to see how well I can love.

I'm called to take care of every need of a person who has provided everything to me while I was growing up, but who has also been a source of unbelievable pain for me in adulthood at times when I most needed her love and understanding. I realized years ago that she and I don't think alike. We have very different world views, and we have different ideas about spirituality and family and loyalty. She does not understand me, and for many years, I've known that she doesn't make any effort to try to understand me. She only wants me to be like her, to think like her, to see the world the way she sees it.

Now, as she is sometimes confused and sometimes sharp as a tack, I see how passive aggressive she can be. And I see that she enjoys being a martyr, and that she has great skill at saying things and making gestures that get me to feel guilty.

Scott has said that he's seen her do things that make her 'unlikeable' at times. She criticizes my choices frequently, on small matters and on significant things.

And she quietly shakes her head in disapproval over even the tiniest things. She comments on everything, and even when her comments are positive, I don't always want to hear them. But she can also be sweet. I know that she loves me, because she says it all the time, and she often says how grateful she is to me. But as much as it pains me to admit it, I just don't enjoy her company and would almost always prefer to be alone or with someone else.

But she's here in my home needing care with every detail of daily living. I change her, and dress her, and help in the bathroom, feeling like I don't really know what I'm doing. In confusion, she has referred to me as her nurse, and she has called me her mother. And in clarity, she has called me a dictator and a general, for things like telling her it's time to put her feet back into the bed.

And that's why I think this must be a test for me from the Universe. It's my chance to put aside all of my collected baggage from the years of experiencing her controlling nature and her fussy demands, and to just do what needs to be done. The question will be, "How did you respond when given this role?" And I want to be able to say that I did my best. But I'm fairly certain that means that I have to stop complaining and just be loving and kind. And patient.

On the two nights when we thought she might be starting to die, I felt peace sitting with her. I felt that our time together like this has been healing and positive. I thought about the countless hours we've spent together in the past few months looking at her books and photos, sorting her belongings, reliving all her stories from her younger years.

I patted myself on the back for responding with kindness even when I'm exhausted and frustrated. I knew she was ready to go to a peaceful place. I knew that I'd miss her and feel relief at the same time. But she bounced back, and here I am writing a litany of complaints. No, I'm not handling this gracefully.

That letter to myself helped me to compartmentalize all that was going on in my life. I looked back at that page many times, trying to remind myself that I still had every opportunity to become more graceful, more gracious. But I struggled. At times, I felt desperate, and my thoughts became dark, envisioning self-harm, because I couldn't envision any relief ahead. I felt like I might never be truly happy again.

Around that time, a friend who happened to be a geriatric psychiatrist, visited with my mother and me a few times and assured me that, while nothing is ever certain, my mother seemed to be looking great for her diagnosis, and he expected that she still had a long time with us. It was good news, meaning that I wouldn't lose her anytime soon, and it was bad news, meaning that she would be with us for quite a while. I didn't envision any relief in the future. This was probably going to be my reality for a long time more.

I also wrote a poem from her point of view, as if she was looking at me. She often spoke about our daily life together, so I knew that she was thinking about it too. She felt that she was *ready to go*, as she'd say, and she didn't want to be the burden that she was so certain she was becoming. But I don't think she had any idea of how things really felt to me.

In my poem, I projected the thoughts and ideas that I'd wondered if she'd actually had. I called it *My Mother's Thoughts (Maybe)*. It was a heartbreaking poem for me to write, but it felt like a balm for me too. Writing it and rereading it helped me to see things like an outsider looking in. It helped me to pretend that things were temporary, and it helped me to keep going as every day was becoming more and more difficult, cycling between her happy, clear moments and her moments of extreme agitation.

Even our routine of walking up the stairs at bedtime had become more grueling. It seemed like she'd forget the purpose as we were climbing those stairs, and she'd stop midway, as I was standing behind her with my hand on her bottom to push her up onto each subsequent step. She'd stand still, refusing to take another step up, pausing for long periods to tell me a story or a joke, just standing still in the middle of the staircase while I waited in place behind her. If I tried to get her moving again, she'd get very angry and tell me to stop being a tyrant.

When we'd finally get to the top and make it to her bedroom, the requests to sit and talk became lengthier too. I'd try to keep things positive and I'd sit with her brushing her hair or rubbing her back, and it sometimes lasted for hours. Sometimes, she'd see her parents, my Oma and Opa, right there in the room with her, and she'd talk to them. More than once, she told me that Oma was holding her hand. She also saw my father in her room.

I used to like to look in the large mirror hanging above her dresser and see the two of us sitting side by side, and I'd imagine the spirits she was seeing being all around us. I believed that she saw spirits, because I felt their presence too. It was a feeling that we weren't really alone in that room, that there were others around us. And sometimes, I felt that I knew exactly who was with us too. It was a calming presence, but I also believed that when I was by myself, I could talk to those spirits candidly.

On one particularly bad evening, when my mother couldn't seem to manage in the bathroom and was becoming very agitated and upset with me, I actually spoke to my father's photo. I picked it up from my mother's dresser while she was brushing her teeth and couldn't hear me, and I whispered angrily to the photo.

"Why aren't you helping her? Why are you letting her live like this? She doesn't like being this way, and I don't know if I can take care of her much longer like this! Why did you leave us?"

I actually started to cry and angrily shook the photo in my hand as I continued to stare at my father's image and quietly begged, "Daddy, help me! Help me to help her! Help me, or take her away! Just do *something*!" Even as I whispered the desperate words, I felt guilty for feeling that way.

And it was just a week later that the steep decline began.

My Mother's Thoughts (Maybe)

When the fact that I woke up today
makes someone sad,
is it time to die?
Seeing her eyes,
I know she's lonely, too.
Her caregiving eyes
avoiding eye contact with me
because she cannot bear to look
at another day
and another day
and another day
of her existence in this box.
Both of us together and alone.
I wake up crying, and I go to sleep
crying.
And I see her looking toward the window as she listens to me,
longing to be out there
somewhere else,
somewhere not my too-warm bedroom
with sheets and wipes and basins,
both of us deep-breathing to get through the days.
Nothing makes sense to me, nothing
is clear.
I wonder who I am now,
what I have become.
In my confusion, I accuse her
I blame her, I stab at her
with words I don't mean, but
sometimes I do mean them. She has the ability

to move, to think
to understand.
I want her every moment,
so I call out,
ask her to stay, to never look away.
I see tears in her eyes, knowing
I hurt her, and I wish
I could run away. Wish
I could run.
And then she looks at me
deeply and patiently
into my eyes
and smiles, a weary effort I see,
but she smiles and we laugh,
and I tell her my stories
over and over and over
hoping she'll value them
hoping she'll remember them, hoping
they'll all remember me
as I was.
I love them.
She kisses my forehead and talks about Daddy
about my children and grandchildren
until I cry again, or whimper
or moan.
She spends our days waiting
on me, waiting for me,
listening to me complain
anticipating my demands.
Please don't resent me. Please
don't leave me.
Her eyes look tired and lost,
as mine feel.
My life is her life now.
I am the cause
of her life

*and our imprisonment in this death-wait will birth us both one day,
on the day I don't wake up.
My daughter
is my mother now.
Her hands on mine
as mine were on hers long ago
when I was not the infant I have grown to be.
I am shrinking from my life,
from all life and from living,
bringing her into my decline,
begging her to stay at my side until the end
and at the end
knowing, trusting that she will be there
still.
She wants peace
for me. She tells me
let go and trust.
I count days on my paper calendar
watching the little boxes and lines
jumble into nonsense.
She won't tell me the plan she doesn't know.
She doesn't know.
There are no answers
no good questions.*

Chapter 7
Saying Goodbye

Mom: "As of today, I am officially a member of the Taj Mahal."
Scott: "What does that mean?"
Mom: "I don't know."

My husband, Scott, and my mother, Ellen, age 93

If leaving's not the hardest part, then it's saying goodbye.

I wrote those words in 1988 when I was about to graduate from college. That line was the beginning of the chorus in the song that I wrote to be sung at our Baccalaureate. After four years on campus, it felt like the most significant rite of passage I'd experienced up to that point, so I wanted to capture the feeling in a song.

I was part of the small group that sang weekly at our Catholic masses on campus, so I was poised to be part of the music for the Baccalaureate, and to my delight, my song was approved to be sung by our folksy group of musicians and singers.

I had thought about those words a lot as graduation approached, that the act of saying goodbye might be harder than the actual leaving. The idea of finding the right words to say to someone at the conclusion of a journey together seemed almost impossible. How could I possibly say goodbye to friends who had shared the same experiences with me?

I'd had a class in my senior year of college entitled *The Philosophy of Creativity and Beauty*, and our capstone project had one instruction; we were told to 'Express beauty creatively'. It was that class and those vague, but amazingly simple, instructions that gave me the idea for the song I wrote. This was going to be a milestone, and I needed to take the time to express meaningful farewells to the people around me, the people I'd come to love.

And as painful and poignant as that effort might be, in the end it would be beautiful to have said goodbye properly.

That same thing was true in so many situations throughout life, and it was true, again, as I lived with my mother. But I didn't realize until well into the process of her final decline that we were already saying our goodbyes.

About two weeks before my mother died, but of course we weren't aware of that timeline, Scott said to me that my mother's recent confusion and agitation reminded him a lot of the way his first wife had behaved in the weeks just before she passed. At mealtimes, my mother would try to maintain conversations but her sentences and phrases were almost nonsensical.

While we had been enjoying her comical quotes during those months together, this wasn't quite so funny anymore. In fact, I'd feel alarmed when it would happen, which was more and more frequently. But Scott's gentle warning still didn't land with me the way it should have. I had strong doubts that my mother was going to pass any time soon.

Just four days before my mother died, a man came to our door soliciting donations for the local Volunteer Fire Department, and my mother was so alert that she called to me from the den while I was talking to him at the front door, and she said that she wanted to give him a check from herself too. She rallied herself to make that offer. If you had told me at that moment that she'd be dead four days later, I would not have believed it. She was different for sure, but she wasn't out of the game.

I thought that maybe her medication needed to be adjusted or changed, and I spoke with the nurse about that. The nurse did feel that there was a change with my mother, but for the most part, her vital signs were still strong. However, during a visit that week, my mother's heart rate was 37 for at least twenty minutes while the nurse was with her. Normal is 60-100.

It went back to 60 just before the nurse left. A few weeks prior to that, her heart rate was 42 when checked by the nurse, but it went right back up to 70 about two minutes later, so it seemed like a fluke.

Usually, her heart rate was around 70. But on that day, it stayed right around 37 for a while. The nurse checked with the hospice doctor, and they both suspected that my mother's heart rate would periodically drop and then come back to normal. The nurse emphasized to me that it did not mean that death is imminent, but it did mean that changes could happen quickly, whenever her time might come.

I did a little bit of research on my own, just to supplement what the nurse and doctor had said, and I learned that if a person has a heart rate below 40 for any amount of time, it's an indication of second or third degree heart block. If they are otherwise healthy, a pacemaker would be needed immediately. With hospice patients, though, they wouldn't withstand the pacemaker surgery, so palliative care would be the right course.

In fact, her doctor back in Pennsylvania had also said that she would not be appropriate for a pacemaker given her age and weakness. It seemed that heart blockage is the type of thing that can cause a quieter and quick death, rather than having patients linger at the end. I could not find any sort of prognosis timeline. I figured that she could still have many months, or it could be weeks or days.

From what the nurse told me, it's generally understood that heart rates don't fall below 40 often, and almost never fall below 30. The nurse said that the heart would likely just stop all together before going that low.

The nurse did say that it was good that my mother's heart rate went back up to 60 on its own. But this was a new observation for her health, so the nurse explained that she was going to continue to monitor my mother's heart rate closely. She also told me that this information was not cause for alarm, because this just might be how my mother's heart was working at this point. My mother could still possibly have a very slow decline.

I kept in close contact with my sisters through texts and phone calls. I told them that there were days when my mother would stay in bed all day, but that even on those days, she usually talked and joked, sometimes coherently and sometimes not, and she occasionally ate light meals in her bedroom.

I thought that my mother might surprise us and hold on for a good while longer. My mother still had her will to be active, even in her confusion. Zoe was home with us then, having completed her sophomore year of college, and one evening I needed to run out for a quick errand. It was around 6 p.m., and my mother had been in bed all day. She hadn't yet found the strength to sit up.

But she had been talking with me and seemed coherent, and I expected that Zoe, who was almost twenty years old, would be able to manage for a half hour as long as I could be reached on my cell phone for emergencies. Zoe had encouraged me to go out myself, to take a break, instead of letting her running the errand for me. She felt confident.

So, I prepared my mother and told her that I'd be heading out for a short time, and when I was ready to actually go out the door, I went back up to her bedroom, where she was still lying with her blankets up to her chin, and said, "I'm leaving now, and I'll be back in just a few minutes, but Zoe is here."

Her grandmotherly response made me smile. "Zoe will be fine. I'll be here with her."

It wasn't long after that when my mother started to have hallucinations. She would see things in the room that weren't there, and she thought that the bathroom floor mats were talking to her. That happened a few days in a row. I'd take her to the bathroom and she'd freeze as soon as she looked down at the bathmats.

"What am I supposed to do with those things on the floor?" she'd ask me. "They're telling me to use them for something."

I didn't understand what she meant, but she said the same thing with every bathroom trip. "They're telling me to use them."

So, I removed the bathmats from both of the bathrooms.

During that week, my mother had again rebounded at times, going through her usual daily routine, although much slower and without getting dressed into daytime clothes. She had taken to wearing her nightgowns throughout the day, covered by a long zippered fleece robe, even though it was already getting warm, because it was May. The effort involved in changing clothes was simply too much for her in the evenings, so I'd instead help her into a fresh nightgown each morning.

I'd put her feet into clean socks with her moccasins, and I'd take her down to the den dressed like that. Then, in the evenings, she didn't have to change clothes again. She could just use the bathroom and get ready for bed.

She'd been able to come downstairs most days, but her visits from the hospice team were becoming more frequent. Sometimes it bothered her to have visitors so often, but at this point, she didn't always remember what day it was, and she definitely didn't remember what had happened the previous day. Her nurse was coming three times a week and her aide was coming five times a week, so every weekday.

My mother was no longer able to make an extra trip up the stairs to go to the shower, so her aide was helping her wash up using a basin in the den. We'd close the drapes for privacy and they'd get to work. The aide was always careful to keep a blanket over my mother while washing her, one part of her body at a time, so that she wouldn't get cold, and my mother seemed to enjoy feeling clean and fresh, despite her newfound daily resistance to getting washed.

She would complain before the aide or the nurse arrived about not wanting people to come. She would say that she wanted them to leave her alone, but when they'd arrive, she's be happy to see the familiar faces of her helpers. And once they'd get started with their usual routine, she'd feel glad that they were there for her. But it was getting more difficult every day to convince her that the hospice team needed to come by. She was just so easily agitated, and she was getting more and more aggressive with me.

For four nights in a row, when we were ready to take her upstairs to bed, I actually had to fully push her up to each step. She was getting too weak to help at all. She'd hang onto the railing and I'd literally lift her foot onto the next step and then push her up. The effort was all mine. Scott or Zoe would have to be behind me so that I wouldn't fall backward.

There was a night when things really frightened me. Actually, I guess I should say that it was a morning, because it was about 4 a.m. when I saw the light go on in my mother's room. I'd become a very light sleeper again, as I had been when my daughters were little, so the change in light woke me. Then, I heard the jingle bells on my mother's walker, so I knew that she was trying to get up, and maybe she was up already. I didn't waste time getting out of bed, but ran down the hallway in my pajamas and bare feet.

I found my mother standing in her room silhouetted by the light from her nightstand lamp. She was leaning on her walker and she was struggling to put on her robe, which we kept folded on the bedside commode that she never used. She was muttering angrily because she was having difficulty getting her arm into the sleeve.

"Help me!" she barked, as soon as I stepped into the room.

"What are you doing?" I asked, still dazed from sleep.

"I'm trying to put this blasted thing on, but it won't work," she said, swinging the sleeve of her robe toward me with one shaky hand. I tried to take the robe from her but she held onto it. It seemed like she wasn't sure whether or not she wanted to give it to me. She pushed and pulled at it until it was just hanging over her walker.

"Do you have to go to the bathroom?" I asked, stepping forward to let her lean on me. "You don't need your robe on for that. Let's just get in there."

"No!" she hollered angrily, stepping away from my outstretched hand. "I don't have to go to the bathroom." She repeated it again, sounding sing-songy, like she was mocking the question I'd asked. "I don't have to *go to the bathroom.*

I'm trying to go downstairs! Help me get this thing on!" She continued, her voice growing louder, as she tugged again at the robe, which was getting tangled around her walker.

"Mom, Zoe is asleep right on the other side of this wall. Can you keep your voice down?"

"I need to go downstairs," she yelled, her eyes darting from one thing to another, like she was searching for something in her room. "Don't tell me to be quiet! Just help me put this on!" She pushed her walker forward, as if she was trying to ram me out of the way.

"Mom, please calm down," I said, feeling my frustration rising, but knowing that she was completely disoriented. "It's not time to go downstairs. It's still the middle of the night."

"It is *not* the middle of the night!" she said, furiously. "You've left me up here all day, and I want to go downstairs. I'm going downstairs *now*."

"I didn't leave you upstairs. I've been in bed sleeping. You were sleeping too. It's night-time. It's still time to be sleeping."

"You left me here, all alone," she continued, yelling full out. "And I want to go downstairs! You think you can just leave me in this room, and you won't listen to me, and you won't come in."

I could see that she was much more agitated and aggressive than usual, and I thought about getting more medicine, but I couldn't leave her alone while I ran to get her prescriptions. I was about to call loudly for Scott or Zoe, but I was afraid that I'd actually make her more upset if I called for them.

"Mom, please take it easy," I begged. I pulled her robe off the walker and laid it across her bed. "Why don't you sit down and we can talk?"

"I don't want to sit down!" She was getting more and more upset with me. "Don't treat me like a child! I want to go downstairs *now*! It's getting late. What time is it?" she asked.

"It's four in the morning," I said, exasperated, but trying to help her understand. "I think maybe you had a dream." I didn't want her to feel ridiculous or embarrassed. "I think maybe you had a dream that woke you up, and you thought that it's morning. But it's not time to get up yet. It's only four in the morning."

"It's four in the morning?" she repeated, her voice all at once sounding timid.

I nodded. "Yes, it's four in the morning. Please sit down with me."

She stared at me and her face instantly became childlike. She stopped looking all around the room and just stood there staring at me, and I could see the realization set in. Her face filled with despair and pleading. I could tell just by looking into those eyes that she felt lost.

She knew on some level that she had made a mistake, so I watched her as she started thinking. She stood there quietly for a few moments, and then her brow wrinkled in concentration, and I knew that she was searching her thoughts, trying to make sense of this. And she tried to save face.

"Well, I'm awake now," she began, her voice back to normal volume. "I'm awake, and I really do want to go downstairs. I can say my prayers and I'll wait for you for breakfast."

"Mom," I said, shaking my head, "it's way too early. I'm really tired. Can't we both just go back to bed and sleep a little more?" But I already knew that I was done sleeping, because even if she did get back into bed to fall asleep again, I'd want to keep an eye on her to make sure she was okay.

"I'll make a deal with you," she offered. "I'll go downstairs, and you can go back to bed."

"I can't do that," I replied, with a sigh. "I'm not going to leave you downstairs alone. It's still dark outside. Scott and Zoe are still asleep too. Let's just both go back to bed."

But she dug in and her stubbornness reared. "I said that I'm going downstairs, and that's what I'm going to do."

"Well, I don't want to take you down there yet," I argued. I could be stubborn too.

"I don't need your help," she insisted. "I can certainly manage to walk downstairs by myself."

"I don't think that's true. I walk with you up and down the stairs every day, every time you use the stairs. You can't go by yourself. Please just sit down."

"I am *not* going to sit down until I'm downstairs." She was getting angry again. "You can't always tell me what to do. I can go down the steps alone. I'll use my walker. I'll use it all the way down the steps." *Seriously?* I could see that this wasn't going to get resolved easily.

"Fine," I gave in. "I'll take you downstairs, but I need to get myself together first. Just give me five minutes to use the bathroom and get some socks for myself. Okay? Sit down for a minute and I'll be right back."

She rolled her eyes at me and made a tsk-tsk noise. "I guess you don't trust me. You don't think I can even walk down steps. I'm a grown woman!"

I just stared at her. "Please…"

"Fine, I'll sit down. Go do what you need to do." And she backed up her walker and sat on the side of her bed.

I dashed back to my room and had just pulled a pair of socks from my drawer when I heard the jingle bells again and knew she wasn't waiting for me. Still barefoot, I started back toward her room, only to see her heading straight toward me, toward the top of the staircase, which was by my bedroom doorway.

"Hey, where are you going? You said you'd give me a minute to get ready?"

"You don't have to get ready. You can go to bed. I can go downstairs by myself. Move over." She tried to push past me with the walker. I had to start walking backward to avoid getting pressed against the wall.

"Mom! Please! Stop for a minute," I implored.

But she kept pushing forward and I kept backing up. There was no way that I was going to stop her without using physical force. My stomach was in knots and I felt like I could cry, but I quickly reached around the corner to put on the bathroom light to brighten the dark hallway, and I just let her keep moving forward.

"You win," I said. "Let's go downstairs. Let's go together."

I flipped on the light for the stairwell and we did our usual walk down the stairs, but she was shaking and weak, and I had to practically carry her down the last few steps. I got her settled in her green recliner and I put her blanket over her lap. She asked me to open the drapes there in the den and I agreed, only because I was too tired to argue any more.

I opened them and she saw that it was dark outside, and I think that she again realized that she was mixed up about time. I encouraged her to put her feet up, and I said that I'd go get her a cup of water from the kitchen and start making her coffee and toast. She finally seemed settled when I left the room.

I was only gone for a minute or two filling one of her plastic mugs with water, but when I came back into the room, she was sound asleep. I went back upstairs to get a sweatshirt for myself as well as my mother's robe, which was still on her bed, and her walker, which was still at the top of the stairs. When I came back to the den, I fell asleep in the chair beside her.

A few times, I opened my eyes and looked over at her resting as peacefully as could be, and I wondered what was going on inside her brain. I was frightened and overwhelmed, and I was very worried about how I could convince her never to try to walk the stairs alone. Eventually, the *real* morning came and she awoke as if she'd just taken a nap in her chair. She didn't seem to remember any of it.

When the nurse visited that day, I told her the story of the 4 a.m. confusion, and that my mother had believed, even if only for a short time, that she could walk down the stairs alone. I told her what my mother had said about using her walker on the stairs, and that she was heading toward the stairs even before I was ready to help her. The nurse made it absolutely clear that it was time to order the hospital bed for the den.

She didn't give me a choice about it, and she didn't give my mother a choice. She only asked me what would be a convenient time for delivery.

My mother also told the nurse that the bathroom mats had been telling her what to do, so the nurse witnessed the confusion first-hand. She stayed for a longer visit than usual that day, monitoring my mother's vital signs the whole time. The nurse said that on this visit my mother's vital signs were inconsistent. Her heart rate changed from 80 to 52, then down to 40, and back to 58, all during that one visit.

She had been seated the whole time, so there was no exertion causing those changes. It was just her heart getting weaker. Her blood pressure was still normal, the nurse said, although it dropped a bit on one of the readings. She emphasized that the steps were no longer safe for my mother, and we went ahead and ordered the hospital bed. It was to be delivered the next morning.

So, that night, my mother slept in her bedroom for the last time, her last night being upstairs. As the nurse had advised, we increased her anxiety medication just a little bit so that she'd sleep more soundly.

After my mother was asleep upstairs, Scott, Zoe and I moved some furniture around in the den. Weeks before, I had mapped out where everything would fit, in anticipation of this day coming. Because the hospital bed was going to be central in the den, we moved the two reclining chairs against the walls. My mother's sideboard from her old dining room set was against another wall, and that would stay in place.

The sideboard would be the surface closest to the hospital bed, so I thought that I might be able to make it look like her dresser. The sideboard had drawers that were filled with my mother's supplies, such as staplers, tape and typewriter ribbons, as well as some table linens and travel albums. On top of the sideboard, she had previously kept some practical items, like a magnifying glass, tissues, a bag of hard candy, and some magazines, to be within easy reach of her usual chair.

I moved all of those things aside and left the surface clear. We also lugged a twin mattress up from our basement and we placed it in the middle of living room floor for me to sleep on, because I'd have to be able to hear my mother at night. It wasn't a great place to have a mattress, but there wasn't any other option. So, we were set for the delivery of the hospital bed the next morning.

My mother slept soundly and didn't wake up during that night, but I didn't sleep anyway. I laid in my own bed, knowing it was my last night upstairs as well, but I was on alert. I probably leaned over and looked down the hallway every half hour to make sure that my mother's bedroom was still dark and that she wasn't walking in the hallway or trying to go downstairs.

I knew that she wasn't too happy about the hospital bed, but when we spoke in terms of danger to all of us on the steps, she came around. I had to remind her that it took two of us to get her up the stairs every evening, and that if she fell, she'd topple me and also Scott or Zoe, depending on who was helping that day. Still, I don't think my mother fully understood that she wouldn't be in her upstairs bedroom any more.

She didn't comprehend that she was very soon going to be completely done with the stairs. We did talk briefly with the nurse about the possibility of keeping my mother in her bedroom around the clock, but there were a few reasons why that wouldn't work. For one thing, I thought it would be better for her to be where the family was all day than to be alone in her room. Also, the hospital bed wouldn't fit up the steps, and she was going to need a bed that could change positions, so the decision was really made based on that.

Despite feeling exhausted over the preparations for it, I believed that the transition to a hospital bed would be a positive thing, because the evenings in the upstairs bathroom had become hellish during that final week. My mother had gotten to the point where she'd started doing and saying things that were too sad to mention to anyone other than the nurse. I knew that I wouldn't be able to handle much more, and I truly hoped that by eliminating the exhausting trips up the stairs each night, my mother might be able to stay more coherent and manage more easily.

The next day, the hospital bed arrived at 9 a.m., and it was exactly in the nick of time.

That morning, my mother woke up and told me that she wasn't sure she felt strong enough to go downstairs. It was going to be another day of staying in her bedroom. So, I brought her breakfast up to her but she barely ate anything. When her aide came that day, and the hospital bed was already waiting in the den, her aide suggested that the two of us together walk my mother down the stairs, and we did.

I took my usual spot on the steps just below my mother, going down the steps backward in front of her with my hands on her side and her bottom, and her aide stayed one step above her, with her hands under my mother's arms, guiding her and holding her.

I had put clean, floral sheets onto the hospital bed, and while her aide was helping my mother to get washed, I quickly ran upstairs and collected most of the small photos and trinkets that my mother kept on her dresser. I quickly set up the top of the sideboard next to the hospital bed to look just like her dresser. I'd brought down the blankets from her bed, and tried to make it look as familiar as possible.

We put the bed into the sitting-up position, and my mother said that it was the most comfortable she'd ever felt. She liked seeing that her dresser items were still beside her, and especially enjoyed having the photos of my father right there. I also added some photos of her grandchildren, and her brand new great-granddaughter. She seemed ready to accept that her bed would be in the den, but she told her aide and me that she still wanted to go upstairs sometimes.

We played along because we didn't want to upset her. But I think that my mother finally knew that her days of walking up the stairs were over.

Although, she settled comfortably into the new bed, she wasn't herself that day. She was hallucinating again, and she told her aide that there was a castle behind the house across the street, and that the castle had pillows for her. She looked very pale and drawn, and later that afternoon, she said that she didn't think she had the strength to walk around the corner to the bathroom. This was completely new.

I suggested that we use the wheelchair that had been parked in the corner of the den ever since she started on hospice. With my help, she was able to sit on the side of the bed, and then I lifted her into a pivot from the bed to the wheelchair. I rolled her in the wheelchair to the bathroom, and she was able to get up, again with my help, and use the bathroom.

Keeping her in the wheelchair after the bathroom trip, I brought some lunch into the den for her, but she had no appetite. She surprised me by needing me to lift her cup of water to her face, so that she could simply put her lips onto the straw to drink. I saw that she was having trouble staying upright in the wheelchair, so I lifted her out and we pivoted her back into the bed. Since she hadn't eaten anything solid, I had another idea.

I had gone out a few days earlier and bought a few cups of my mother's favorite dessert, Wendy's chocolate Frosty. The closest Wendy's restaurant was several miles away, so I had timed my trip when Scott and Zoe could both be home with her. I had wanted so badly to get those for her, because I knew how much she loved them, and I felt like I might not have too many more chances to bring her a treat. It was a love offering. So, knowing we still had a few in the freezer, I got her back into the hospital bed and then offered her a Frosty.

"Ooh, yes!" she said, immediately perking up.

I sat on the side of her bed feeding each tiny spoonful to her until she'd eaten about half of the little cup. She smiled in delight. Zoe came in to sit with us and she thought it was adorable that her grandmother was having a Frosty as a meal. But I think we both knew that this wasn't a good sign. We didn't realize at the time that the Frosty would be her last meal.

That night, Scott and Zoe found things to do upstairs because the lights would be going out in the living room a lot earlier than usual. I got myself set up to sleep on the twin mattress in our living room, but before I turned out the lights, my mother and I still did our usual little dialogue at bedtime.

"Sleep tight, Mommy. I love you," I said as I leaned down to gently hug her.

"Good night. I love you too," she replied, in a whispery voice. "You're my good friend."

She slept soundly but she moaned occasionally, and I went into the den a few times during the night to stand beside her and hold her hand. Silently, I told her that I loved her, and I felt like my heart was speaking to her heart.

The next morning was shocking to me. I came into the den and spoke with her when I saw her eyes open, but she didn't speak to me. She just smiled a weak smile. I asked her if she wanted me to take her to the bathroom, and she simply said, "Uh huh." So, I sat her up, having to practically lift her into a seated position because she was so weak, and pivoted her into the wheelchair the same way I'd done the day before.

She was barely able to help me, so it was much more difficult, but we did it, and I rolled the chair to the bathroom door. She just smiled at me and sat there. She showed no sign at all of wanting to get out of the chair.

"Okay," I said, "let's get you into the bathroom."

But as I tried to lift her to pivot her into the bathroom, I realized that she wasn't able to help at all, meaning that she was a dead weight in the wheelchair. I would have to use all my strength to try to completely lift her and hold her up, and I didn't think I could do that safely.

After lifting her only a few inches from the seat, I gently set her back down in the wheelchair. Scott was at work and Zoe was still asleep upstairs. I didn't think Zoe would hear me if I yelled for help, and I decided that I couldn't leave my mother alone in that wheelchair while I ran to get Zoe. I was afraid that she might fall out of the wheelchair.

"Can you wait a little bit longer to use the bathroom?" I asked her. "I don't think I can lift you alone. I'll get Zoe in a minute, and I'll call the nurse."

My mother nodded her consent, still silent.

So, I rolled her back to the den. My mind was racing. *What should I do?*

"Are you hungry?" I asked her, and she gave a weak nod. I had prepared her toast and jelly before I came in to get her out of bed, so I only had to grab her plate and cup from the kitchen table, and I got back to the den as quickly as possible. As I'd been doing for the past couple of weeks, I had cut her toast and jelly into bite size pieces that she could eat with her special thick-handled fork, which was easier to hold.

But on this day as she sat in the wheelchair, she shook her head when I tried to hand her the fork. She just didn't have the energy to move her arm. I tried to feed her a tiny piece but her jaw was shaking, and she was trembling more than chewing. I held a napkin in front of her so that she could spit it out.

Then, she shook her head. *'No more.'* I tried to give her some water, and she took the tiniest sip before turning her head away.

I took a deep breath and put her plate and cup onto the floor. I knew that it was imperative that I get her back into the bed, and I also had to make an urgent call to the nurse.

"Okay, Mommy, we're going to get you back in bed," I explained. "I'm going to lift you to stand up and you just try to help me, if you can, so that we can pivot you around and get you sitting on the bed. Okay?"

She nodded, weakly.

I don't know why I forgot to call Zoe for help. I think that my mind was racing, and I was both panicked and in a little bit of shock. I just wanted to get my mother back into the bed quickly so that she wouldn't fall out of the wheelchair onto the floor.

I put my arms under hers and used everything I remembered about body mechanics to move someone who was a dead weight. It was almost impossible for me to lift her. After all the times I'd lifted her and supported her, this felt completely different. With gritted teeth and total determination, I finally was able to pull her up into a partially standing position right next to the bed, and she sort of collapsed forward onto me.

I turned her as quickly and gently as I could, with my arms hugging her tightly, and attempted to sit her onto the bed. But she fell backward onto the bed, unable even to hold herself sitting up, and with my arms still around her, I fell too. I landed just beside her, thankfully not landing on top of her, but she cried out in pain from hitting the bed so suddenly. Slowly, I tried to shift her into a better position by pulling the bedsheets, and I put her legs up into the bed. As soon as she was settled, as best as I could manage, I called the nurse.

I told the nurse that my mother seemed very different, not eating or drinking, not talking, and I explained that I couldn't even get her into the bathroom. She assured me that she'd be over within the hour, and she told me not to worry, that my mother could be catheterized. *Oh, no.* I knew that my mother would hate that.

But to my surprise, when the nurse stood at my mother's bedside and explained that she was going to insert a catheter so that my mother could stay in bed, my mother nodded her head with acceptance and resignation. I had to help the nurse by holding my mother's knees, because my mother couldn't even move her own legs. It was the lowest point for me, standing there while the nurse did her work. I closed my eyes, because I thought that my mother might be looking up at me, and I wanted her to see that I respected her privacy.

It was awful knowing that my mother needed a catheter, but it was also a huge relief because it was one less thing that I'd have to worry about. I wouldn't have to take her to the bathroom, although I knew that I still might have to change her, if needed.

Zoe had come down to the kitchen while the nurse was there, but I had texted Zoe from the den when I first heard her walking around upstairs and told her what had been going on that morning. I told her that her grandmother was having an especially bad day, and that I was having trouble moving her around. So, Zoe knew to stay in the kitchen unless we called her. As soon as the nurse was through with the catheter, I went to talk with Zoe while the nurse finished her work with my mother. I told Zoe that it was probably going to be a rough day.

I had no idea exactly how rough it would be.

I went back into the den and I could hardly believe it when the nurse told me that my mother's vital signs were still okay. *How could that be possible?* It added to my confusion, and to my belief that my mother might still rebound. But before the nurse left, she told me that she'd plan to visit again tomorrow. She stopped and patted my mother's shoulder for a few moments, smiling at her. My mother stared back at her and smiled. I wondered if she was saying goodbye.

Throughout that day, my mother mostly slept. She refused anything to eat or drink, and she wasn't talking much at all. She took one spoonful of a Frosty in the mid-afternoon. I followed the instructions I'd been given about her medication, and she seemed to be comfortable, but it was sort of surreal.

For a short time early in the day, she started to speak and kept saying, "We have to plan the wedding." I wondered if she meant that we should be planning the funeral, her funeral, with all of her plans and paperwork. But she also said that she was worried about the wedding rings, so it might have just been another disoriented rambling.

During the day, I kept in close contact with my sisters through phone calls and texts, and I also texted two friends for any helpful advice they could offer. One was the local friend who was a geriatric psychiatrist, and the other was my college roommate and dear friend, who was a former hospice nurse. Both of them told me that I was doing everything correctly, and they assured me that I was handling things as well as could be.

Ironically, one of my main activities during that day, while my mother was sleeping so much, was that I was writing the eulogy for someone else. One of my close friends from childhood had been in touch the day before to tell me that her own mother had died, and she asked me if I'd be able to help her compose something that she could read at her mother's funeral. I knew the family well, so I was glad to be able to help.

When I told her what was going on with my own mother, she offered to find someone else to help her, but I said that I'd do it. I felt like it was sort of cathartic to be working on a eulogy for a friend's mother, while not knowing what was ahead for my own mother. I felt like it was a bizarre sort of emotional preparation for me.

Late in the afternoon, my mother had been asleep for most of the day, and it was apparent that she wasn't bothered by noises or movement or light, but Scott and Zoe and I continued to whisper and tiptoe around. After all the times that I'd wished for some privacy in our home, without my mother interrupting so many conversations, it seemed strange and upsetting to have the house to ourselves as she stayed in the bed in the den.

As I sat alone with her in the evening, I felt a strong spirit presence. I decided to pull one Tarot card, just to see what I might find, and the card I pulled from the deck was The Sun. The Sun's meaning is that all will work out, that things will be okay. It's a card that promises that better things are ahead and that life is good. I wondered if that message was for me or for my mother, but I think it was probably for both of us.

That evening, when I turned out the light in the den, I whispered, "Sleep tight," but she didn't respond. She was already sleeping, tightly and well.

During the night, I heard her breathing change. It became loud and raspy, and it frightened me. I wondered if it might be what's called a *death rattle*, when someone is approaching their last few days. I checked on her frequently, and each time, I whispered to her that I loved her, even though I knew she didn't hear me.

In between checking on her, I laid on my mattress crying. I didn't know what those horrible sounds coming from her meant. Those definitely weren't snores. But as I laid there with my fear and anxiety, I thought that maybe I really did know exactly what was happening.

In the early morning hours, while it was still dark outside, I used my cell phone to type out a poem. I was lying on my back on the mattress, holding the phone above me when I started the poem, but by the time I finished, I was curled on my side with tears running down my face.

Still, I knew that my mother had rebounded so many times. I thought that maybe she'd bounce back again, that these were just some difficult days. If her time was coming, I wanted to say goodbye beautifully, but I just didn't know what to believe. I was completely worn out and feeling overwhelmed, and my sense of the future just wasn't clear.

I think that I was too close to really see it. With other people, family members or friends or patients through hospice, when I've had the honor of being near them in their last days, I could see it so clearly. I knew the signs and symptoms of active dying. But with my own mother, I just didn't recognize what was happening right in front of me.

I didn't have time to step back and look at her clearly, because, I think, maybe part of me was also about to die.

Death Rattle

*I hear her exhaling her life
in the next room.
I've been listening
all night long
to the irregular rhythm
of the gurgles and moans
as I lay on a mattress
on the living room floor.
Her hospital bed came just in time,
twenty four hours
before she couldn't walk
couldn't talk
couldn't be my mother
any more.
Vital signs strong
says the hospice nurse,
but I know I hear death in her throat,
in the air all around her.
The darkness masks the signs of life
and that sound, those sounds,
slice through the house
disrupting and disturbing.
No more peaceful sleep
no sweet dreams.
I silently go to her several times
peeking in, sitting in her darkness,
holding her hand as she sleeps.
But I don't want to startle,
so I slink back to my spot*

and try to rest,
knowing that the sound she makes
with each labored breath
marks my own mortality,
too.

Chapter 8
Her Last Day

"I'm not afraid of dying. I'm ready to go."

My mother, Ellen, age 93

As I got up off that mattress from another night of barely sleeping, even after my night-long vigil and litany of fears, I still was not completely convinced that it was going to be my mother's last day of earthly life. One of my deepest regrets is that I didn't realize sooner how close she was to the end. I might have treated the whole day with reverence, but that realization only began for me late in the afternoon, when the situation was spelled out for me.

Some details of that day seem fuzzy and distorted, but other details are still strangely crisp and clear. I moved through parts of that day as if it was a blur, and at other times, I knew I'd never forget exactly where I was sitting or standing, exactly what sounds were in our house, exactly what degree of darkness had crept through the windows as the day wore on toward night. I'd remember the odors, the busy-ness, the stillness, the numbness. I'd remember the tears. I'd hold onto all of it.

My mother was still asleep when the nurse called me in the morning. The nurse's visit that day would be in the afternoon, but she called early to check in. She asked if I'd like to have some more support that day. I said that it would be nice to have a hospice visitor or two, especially since my mother was sleeping so much. We had previously scheduled a visit for my mother that day with the nun who did outreach to people who were homebound within the Catholic parish, but I didn't know if my mother would be awake for that.

The nurse also suggested, and I agreed, that it would be a good idea to ask the parish priest to visit as well. I told the nurse that I had actually called for a priest just a week earlier, on a day when my mother was feeling very weak, and that he had come to our home and given her the sacrament of Anointing of the Sick. But I knew that a person can receive that sacrament more than once, so I felt that it would be something my mother would appreciate. She always felt better when a priest was visiting.

During that morning, my mother wasn't waking up for more than a minute at a time. She refused water. She didn't look good at all. She barely spoke, and when she did mumble something, we couldn't really understand what she was trying to say. I started to suspect that maybe she was slowing down for good, that this might really be the final decline.

The medicine seemed to keep her comfortable, and I was using a dropper to put the liquid prescriptions into her mouth as needed. The hospice also gave me lemon swabs to rub on her lips and in her mouth to help moisten her mouth. She didn't seem like she was in any pain at all. In fact, she seemed calm and peaceful, but I thought that maybe we should start to prepare ourselves for whatever might be ahead in the next few days.

I contacted my sisters and told them that they could come if they were able. Both of them started looking into possibilities for travel, but I didn't have a sense of how long my mother still had. I kept paging through the papers that the hospice had given me back at the beginning, trying to figure out where she was in the stages of approaching death. I also looked online, wishing that I could get a definite answer about exactly what to expect.

The priest showed up within the hour and I greeted him at the door. It was a different priest than the one who had visited the week before. I quickly told him that my mother's hospice nurse thought that we should call him, and he didn't delay but walked quickly into the den and went right to her bedside.

"Mom," I said, in a slightly raised voice, hoping to rally her a little. "Father is here to pray with you and anoint you."

She opened her eyes immediately and looked at him, but she closed her eyes quickly again. But I knew that she saw him. He began to pray with her, standing to the right side of her bed, and I stood on the left side, with my hand holding her left hand. When the priest began the traditional words, "In the name of the Father, and the Son and the Holy Spirit…," my mother moved her right hand into the air, lifting it about ten inches off the blanket, probably instinctively.

It was like an automatic response to those words; she wanted to bless herself, beginning with her right hand touching her forehead. She couldn't move her arm that much, but it was clear that she tried. That little bit of arm movement was the most she had moved on her own since the night before.

The three of us prayed together. When the priest started to say the words of the Lord's Prayer out loud, I joined in and said them out loud too. My mother, I felt certain, was following along silently. The priest then began the ritual for anointing her, and as he was speaking and gently rubbing the oil onto her forehead with his thumb, she mumbled something, still with her eyes closed. A moment later, she started her labored breathing again, and clearly had fallen back to sleep.

As the priest concluded his prayers, he remained very quiet. It felt like a sort of reverence for this sacred time of her life, her passing over into death. He didn't speak as he put his things back into his small leather bag, but as he walked toward me and toward the front door to leave, he simply reached out and hugged me. He didn't say a word, just hugged me.

And I thought to myself, *he knows she's dying soon*. Then he opened the door and quietly left. I was grateful that he didn't try to say any words of consolation to me, and that he didn't tell me to call if I needed anything. His silence spoke more. He was emotional too. The hug was enough. It was just right for that moment.

The social worker came shortly after the priest left. She and I sat together in my mother's two chairs in the den, as my mother lay quietly in the hospital bed next to us. We chatted about the changes that had been observed in my mother during the last few days, and she asked if I was doing okay. I told her that I had my routine with my mother, but that everything had changed since yesterday.

I still had that clinging fear that if my mother got any worse, I wouldn't be able to handle it at home, but the social worker told me that she believed I'd be okay. Even then, I didn't really make the connection. I didn't understand that she was telling me she didn't think my mother's struggle would last much longer. We sat for almost an hour, mostly talking about me and my support system.

She asked how Scott and Zoe were handling things. She asked about Abby, living at a distance. And she reminded me that when the time comes, there would be bereavement services available.

During the late morning and early afternoon, recognizing that my mother wasn't doing well, I encouraged my sisters and niece and nephews to call if they wanted to talk with her. Abby called too, from Salt Lake City, as she often did. But this time, Abby didn't get to have a pleasant chat with her grandmother, as she was used to. Each time someone called, I put my cell phone on the speaker setting and held it close to my mother's ear so that she could hear the voice easily.

I'd tell her who it was and she'd blink her eyes. I am certain that she heard each of them, although she wasn't able to talk. She just listened.

I did feel myself having a momentary giggle, though, when one of my family members began the call by saying to my mother, "Hi! What's new?"

When the response was silence, I said, "She hears you but she can't answer." The family member did quickly recover composure and just continued to talk, with messages of love and prayers. And despite my inappropriate giggle, I understood. It was so easy to be at a loss for the right words to say.

In the early afternoon, the hospice chaplain made her regular visit, but a day earlier than had been previously scheduled, and she arrived at just about the same time as the nun from the local parish. The two of them greeted each other, and I realized that the chaplain had called the parish during the day to make sure that a priest had been sent to visit. So, the nun had actually spoken to the chaplain before arriving at our house.

It seemed like maybe they had planned their approach, because the nun asked me if I'd like to sit with her in the living room, while the chaplain visited with my mother in the den. We talked quietly. The nun never asked me if I was Catholic and we didn't talk about religion at all. She wanted to know how I was coping with caring for my mother. She asked about my family, and we talked about music, because she had admired my mother's piano.

She walked over to look at the sheet music book that was still sitting on the piano from the last time that my mother had played it, and the nun told me that she owned the very same book. After about a half hour of quiet conversation, she went in to see my mother, but very briefly, and then she went on her way.

Zoe had gone to the gym, and Scott was at work, because none of us realized the magnitude of the day we were in. So, it was just me and the chaplain and my mother for a little while. I sat down on the bench by the window while the chaplain stayed by my mother's side.

"I was just playing her some music," she said to me. "I found some pieces that I thought she'd enjoy."

She showed me her phone and she had put together a short playlist for my mother of Catholic hymns sung in German, and also some classical music. I was deeply touched by this thoughtful and kind gesture. I could hardly speak. After I looked at the list, she took the phone back and started the music again, at a very low volume, and she placed it on the hospital bed next to my mother's pillow. I wished that I had thought of doing something so lovely for my mother, and I wished I had done it sooner.

As we sat there together, we talked in whispers. "How are you holding up?" she asked me.

"Well, that's the question of the day," I replied. "I'm okay, but it's just funny because everyone is asking me how I am today. I guess it's because her situation has changed and everyone's checking to see if I can handle it."

"I think it's more that we've all heard the nursing report," she clarified, "and we all understand these sudden changes with your mom. We all just want you to know that we're here to support you."

"Thank you," I said, quite sincerely. "I really do feel that. And I appreciate it."

"And we do know that you can handle it. No one's worried about that," she said, echoing the social worker's words from a few hours earlier. "So, how are you feeling?"

"Well, I wish I knew what to expect. I mean, I can see that she's struggling, but her vital signs are still okay, I guess. They were okay yesterday, and we'll see what the nurse says this afternoon. So, I'm wondering if she's going to rally again. Yesterday, she did have a few times when she came around for a bit."

"I don't know," the chaplain said, thoughtfully. "She doesn't look like she's going to rally."

"I guess I know that too," I admitted, "but I'm not sure how long she's going to hang on."

"Have you talked to your sisters?" the chaplain asked, knowing that they both lived at a distance.

"Yes, I told them everything that's been going on, and I told them that they can come here if they want to. But I don't know if I should be telling them to rush. I mean, she could hang on for days or weeks."

The chaplain gave a sort of shrug. "Maybe," she said, "but I don't think she has weeks. I'd tell them to come sooner if they can."

I raised my eyebrows. "Really?"

"Yeah," she affirmed. "I'd tell them that if anyone can come right away, they should."

"So," I asked, fearing the answer, "you think she only has a few *days* left, not weeks?"

"Yes." Now she was trying to be gentle, but emphatic. "I'd say she only has days. Or hours."

Hours? Did she just say hours?

Oh my god! Oh my god! I felt my breath catch.

The chaplain stayed seated but I think she saw the realization hit me. "Do you want me to call anyone?" she offered.

"It's okay, I'll tell them. I'll tell them right now."

I walked into the living room, feeling like my legs were no longer attached to my body, and I started calling and texting the whole family, including my sisters, Scott and Abby. I knew Zoe would be home soon. And as I conveyed this information, I felt a wave of surreal emotion, as if I was operating outside of myself, feeling disconnected and numb, yet knowing that I might burst open at the slightest touch.

Just as I was finishing my calls and texts, my mother's aide arrived. I looked at her carefully as she walked into the den to see if she'd say or do anything that might be confirmation of what the chaplain had said. And she most definitely did.

"Oh, look at you!" she said to my mother, seeming shocked, as soon as she came into the room. "What happened here?" She said it gently, but also showing some emotion.

"You think she looks different from yesterday?" I asked.

"Oh, yeah," she said, and she made eye contact with the chaplain. "She's turned a corner, I think."

It's true, I thought. *She's dying in a few hours.*

"Well, we'll get her cleaned up a little bit," her aide continued, "but I don't think we'll do too much today. We don't want to disturb her too much."

I walked the chaplain to the door, after she bent her head and whispered to my mother, gently touching her hair. She hugged me before she left too.

The aide finished her work much more quickly than usual, and she also spoke softly to my mother before leaving. She was more matter-of-fact with me, and she said, "I hope I'll see you tomorrow, but let me know if anything changes." She smiled warmly and left me alone with my mother for the first time that day.

After what seemed like a parade of visitors, I was glad to have a little time to just sit quietly at my mother's side. Unfortunately, my phone was still pinging and ringing with family members asking questions and trying to decide whether or not they could travel to our house quickly enough. My middle sister and her son decided to start driving, but my other sister was simply too far away to make it in time.

I also knew, and advised them all, that they would likely have to travel within the next week or so for a funeral. Both of my sisters had come to visit my mother during the five months that she was with me, and both phoned her every few days, so I hoped that they had no regrets. The distance just couldn't be helped, and they both talked with her often. She loved those phone calls because she adored both of them.

Abby and a few other family members also texted repeatedly to check to see if my mother might be able to talk again, but she couldn't. She hadn't rallied at all. Of course, they also asked for updates and offered support to me. There were a few points during that day when I wished I didn't have to be so distracted by the cell phone, but then I realized that at least I was able to be with my mother and see things first hand, so I tried to get past my dismay at having to check my phone so frequently.

I gave out as much information as I could, as often as I could, and I tried to hold myself together enough to continue to do that.

The nurse arrived later in the afternoon, and she told me that my mother had apnea, which was new for her, so it meant that her breathing was stopping and starting. I told her what the chaplain had said about only having a few hours left, and she said that she expected the same, although these things could never be certain. Before she left, she reviewed with me what to do at the time of death, if that should happen during the night.

I knew to call the hospice first and the on-call nurse would come. I understood from my hospice work, as many people don't understand, that death is not an emergency. Once the person dies, there's no need to rush. That's the time to slow down, to take in the moment and give yourself time to process what's happened. So, I was okay with the knowledge that my mother might pass while we were with her, probably without any of the hospice professionals on hand at that moment.

I also had the contact information for the funeral home ready, as the nurse advised, just so that I wouldn't have to flounder around looking for it later. And because I was my mother's daughter and she had taught me well, I had things completely organized.

The late afternoon and evening had a different feel. Scott came home from work early after my call, and Zoe was with us, and I'm sure we ate something for dinner, but I have no memory of that. We must have taken turns eating. I wanted to stay in the den with my mother as much as possible, so I only stepped out to use the bathroom, or when my phone rang or pinged.

My mother's labored breathing continued, and it was indeed the death rattle sound. With the lights dim, the sound of her gurgled breaths gave the house an eerie, otherworldly feeling.

By early evening, I was finally fully convinced that there wasn't much time left. I felt the presence of spirits all around the room as I sat watching her sleep. I felt that there were many of them all around us, even leaning on the walls and holding onto the ceiling. It was a very loving feeling, and I knew that my mother's entourage was waiting for her.

More than anything, I felt my father in that room, and I felt my Oma and Opa. I felt them as clearly as if they'd been sitting next to me in life, as if I could say something to them and might actually hear their voices answer.

I started to remember what it had been like when my grandparents died, back when my mother was the caregiver. On the day that Opa passed, which was less than a week before my seventeenth birthday, we'd spent an ordinary August day, with me home for summer vacation. Opa hadn't gotten out of bed that day, except to use the bathroom with my mother's help, but he had been sitting up, talking and eating.

Oma spent most of the day sitting in a wicker armchair that my mother had squeezed into the room, pulled forward between the two twin beds, so that Oma could spend her day with her husband of sixty-seven years. In the late afternoon, when my mother and I were spending some time with them in Opa's room, he said that more than anything, he'd like to have a butter cookie. He was diabetic, so he hadn't had his cookies in years. My mother and I were together in the kitchen a short time later, and she looked at me as if she was deep in thought.

"I'm wondering if we should just give him some cookies," she said, inviting my opinion.

"I don't see why not," I answered. My grandfather was ninety-two years old and had dementia and heart disease.

"I think so too," she continued, still debating with herself. "He misses having them and he's always loved cookies." She reached for the cookie box and pulled two out of it. She wrapped them in a napkin and told me to deliver them to him.

He was so delighted to have those cookies that he started to sing an old Viennese folk song, *Oh Du Lieber Augustin*, known for being a song of hope. He sang happily and waved one hand in the air as if conducting an invisible choir. That memory is so clear for me.

About two hours later, my grandmother called out and my mother rushed up the stairs. I heard my mother a moment later crying out, "Oh, Pop! No!" I ran up the stairs and into the room and he was in the bed lying flat on his back breathing loud, raspy breaths.

"Call an ambulance!" my mother ordered me, so I practically flew down the steps to the rotary phone in the dining room. Luckily, my mother kept the emergency phone numbers written on a paper on the small desk top, right next to the phone. I dialed as quickly as I could, my fingers shaking as I waited for each rotary number to finish, which was painfully slow.

After I gave all the information to the dispatcher, I ran back upstairs. Both my mother and my Oma were slumped over his bed crying, each holding one of his hands. His breathing was still loud and sounded like he was blowing raspberries. I could tell, just by instinct, that he was dying.

Having been trained well by my mother about all the Catholic beliefs and traditions surrounding death and dying, I quickly ran into my own bedroom and grabbed the little ribbon of medals that my mother had tied to my bedpost years earlier. I brought it into the room and I placed it in Opa's hand, the hand that my mother had been holding. I'd been taught that if a person dies while holding or wearing a Miraculous Medal, which is a special medal for the Blessed Mother Mary, then that person would go immediately to heaven.

I was a little bit proud of myself for thinking of that. A few moments later, Opa stopped breathing, but none of us said anything. Oma just cried softly, and my mother released an audible anguished sob.

The ambulance arrived a short time later, and I ran downstairs to let them in. I stayed downstairs because the upstairs bedroom and hallway was crowded. Shortly after they'd arrived, they came back downstairs, having made a call to the funeral home instead.

I went back upstairs and Oma was still bent over Opa, but my mother had stepped back a bit. I hugged her and I showed her that I'd placed my medals in his hand. I thought that it would give her solace.

"That was very sweet of you," she said to me, through her tears, "but, you know he wasn't Catholic."

I'd completely forgotten that detail in the chaos. Yes, I knew that Opa was Lutheran, because he was the one who stayed with me on Christmas Eve when everyone older than me went to midnight mass. He used to drive Oma and my mother to church, but he didn't go in. And my mother had a million anecdotes about Opa helping out in the parish, even though he wasn't Catholic.

He did it to support his wife and daughter. I immediately felt silly for having brought the medals to his deathbed. But I also felt confused. If the medals had that power with Catholics, wouldn't they work for everyone else too?

I thought about all of this while my mother was lying on the hospital bed in our den, which was her deathbed now. She wore a Miraculous Medal always, one that my father had given to her. She had asked me to take it off her just a few days earlier, because I think that she was worried that it might wind up in the hands of the funeral director. She wanted to make sure that it was safe to be given to my eldest sister.

So, it was resting on the sideboard next to her, exactly as she'd wanted, so she was covered by the power of the medal, as she believed. I didn't have to put anything into her hands, as I'd tried to do for Opa.

On the night Opa died, my father was home from work by the time the funeral home people arrived. They came into our house soaking wet from the pouring rain, with the hearse double-parked on our Northeast Philadelphia street. I sat in the living room with Oma, holding one of her hands, with my other arm around her shoulder, as they brought Opa's body down the steps on a stretcher.

His head was bobbing slightly under the blanket, and it looked like he was moving, like maybe he was still alive under that blanket. Oma didn't speak at all.

I ate spaghetti—I remember it clearly—with my parents at the kitchen table that evening, and I could see Oma sitting in the living room alone, looking out the window into the dark rainy night. None of us ate much. We were forcing ourselves to seem normal, although my mother couldn't stop crying.

Later that evening, as we were getting ready for bed, my mother was with Oma in what had suddenly become a bedroom for only her. For the second time that day, I heard my mother cry out. I ran to the doorway and Oma was lying back on her bed, as if she'd fallen backward from a sitting position. Her eyes were rolling up and my mother was kneeling beside her sobbing, "No, Mom! Not you too!"

This time, the routine was familiar. I sprinted down the steps, past my father who was on his way upstairs to help. I again called the ambulance, and I began by saying, "You were here earlier today, but we need you again."

Oma died in the hospital a month later, on an evening when my mother and I had been with her in her room and then taken a break for dinner. She passed while she was alone in the room, which was probably the way she wanted it. She'd been in the hospital for an entire month. She never returned home after the night Opa died, after she had a massive heart attack at age eighty-nine. We visited her every day. Some days, she was lucid, and some days she was confused.

On the day of Opa's funeral, Oma obviously couldn't go. The funeral was touching, but it was brief because the family and guests knew that we needed to get to the hospital immediately after the burial. I remember that when we arrived at the funeral home for the viewing just before the funeral service, we saw Opa in his open casket. He was wearing the grey suit that my mother had selected, but my mother was a tiny bit annoyed at first because she had requested a white rose to be placed in his lapel. Instead, it was pink.

My mother asked the funeral director about it and he explained that the white roses didn't look as fresh, and he hoped that the pink would be okay. He offered to switch to a white flower but my mother said that she actually thought the pink rose looked very nice against the grey suit, even though he had never worn that combination.

Following the burial, my parents, my sisters and I went directly to the hospital. Oma was sitting up in bed, having just finished her lunch. As we came in the door, she looked very happy to see us. She obviously didn't realize that we'd just come from her husband's funeral, and we weren't going to tell her.

"I'm so glad you're all here!" she said, with more enthusiasm than we'd heard from her in days. "It's a shame you didn't come a few minutes earlier, though. Pop was just here for a visit and he looked so nice. He was wearing his grey suit but he had on a pink rose instead of a white one. We had such a nice time talking but then he said he had to go. He said it was time to go."

We were all dumbstruck. One of my sisters had to walk out into the hospital hallway to collect herself. It was absolutely amazing to realize that while the rest of us were taking care of our earthly business of ritual and ceremony, Opa had spent the morning with his love. Of course, he was there with Oma while the rest of us were at his funeral.

I remembered those days as we kept vigil with my mother. As the evening wore on, Scott and I sat side by side, sometimes holding hands. Zoe sat with us too, all of us hugging each other at times, and we rotated seats, taking turns being by my mother's side. I pulled the green recliner closer to her bed so that I could sit right beside her.

I felt weary and I wanted to close my eyes too, but I didn't want to fall asleep. I wanted to guard her, to protect her, to see her off whenever the moment came.

My sister and nephew checked in a few times from the road, and we expected them to arrive to our house around midnight. Each time they called, we told them that she was still hanging on, but barely. Eventually, they called to say that they'd arrive around 11 p.m., because they were hurrying on their long drive down the highway.

My mother's breathing continued to punctuate the stillness of the house. The lights were dim and we sat quietly with her. A few times, we spoke with each other, but my mother remained still, in a deep sleep. And despite the disconcerting breathing sounds, she seemed peaceful and pain free.

Shortly after 9 p.m., Zoe came into the den after having been in the kitchen, and she started to speak to me and Scott. She was standing close to the head of the hospital bed, and as she started to speak, she interrupted herself.

"Hey, her eyes are open!" Zoe said.

Scott and I both sprang out of our seats and moved forward until we touched the bedside.

My mother's eyes were indeed open.

"Hi, Mommy," I said, just loud enough that I'd be sure she could hear me without startling her. "We're here with you. I'm here, and Scott and Zoe are here. We love you."

I was leaning over with my left hand on her right shoulder, and my right hand on top of her hand as it rested on her belly. Scott stood slightly behind me, to my right, and Zoe was to my left, just at the head of her bed. My mother moved her eyes back and forth, looking at each of us. Scott and Zoe both spoke to her gently, saying that they loved her.

For a few seconds, I wasn't sure if she was rallying again, or if this might actually be her last moment. From my experience, I knew that many dying people have a last little burst of energy just moments before they pass, so I quickly realized that this was probably what was happening. I felt incredibly happy and incredibly sad, both emotions completely intertwined.

She was looking at us, making eye contact, but it became clear very quickly that she still couldn't speak. She was able to move her head slightly to keep looking from one to another of us.

Then her eyes settled on me. She stared at me. "I love you, Mommy," I whispered.

To my complete surprise, she opened her mouth and started to move her tongue as if she was saying the letter 'L'. She didn't make any sound, but it appeared that she was silently trying to say something that began with 'L'. It continued for a few seconds, as she continued to stare at me.

But I knew what she was saying.

"Are you trying to say you love me? You love us?" And as quickly as I asked, she stopped struggling, stopped moving her mouth and trying to speak. I'd given her the words she wanted to say. She blinked her eyes as if in acknowledgment, and stared at me again.

"I love you too. We all love you. I'll tell the whole family that you said you love us all." She blinked her eyes again.

"Mommy, it's okay to go. It's okay to let go. I'm so glad that you've been here with us, but we'll be okay now. You can let go when you need to. I love you so much. I love you. But you can go be with Daddy whenever you're ready."

As I finished saying those words, she looked past the three of us to a fixed point just past Scott, and I believe that she saw my father standing there too. She stared at that spot for a moment.

Then, she closed her eyes and was gone.

We stood silently—me, Scott and Zoe. Still leaning over her. Still waiting, just in case.

After a few minutes, Zoe silently mouthed to me, "Is she dying?" I nodded my head.

I don't know how much time passed before I stood up straighter and said, "I think she's gone." We hugged each other and cried. After a moment or two, Scott offered to call the hospice nurse. When she arrived about fifteen minutes later, we told her that the time of death had been 9:50 p.m. Scott had remembered that we were supposed to try to look at the clock, if we could, and he'd done that.

While Scott had been calling the nurse, I made calls to my sisters, and Zoe called Abby.

That part is a blur to me. I remember the emotion but not the words. My sister and nephew arrived about an hour later, completely devastated about not making it in time. But I was so glad that they were there. So many of our family members couldn't be there that night due to the distance, but I knew that we were all joined together by something outside of ourselves. We were all connected that night.

The hospice nurse had prepared my mother's body a bit before my sister arrived, and after we all had time to be with my mother, we called the funeral director. They came fairly quickly, and Scott and I stood in the den as they prepared to carry my mother from our house. I felt like my job wasn't over until I saw her safely into their care.

"Do you want to keep these bedsheets?" the funeral director asked me, as they were getting started.

"Yeah, sure," I said, like an automatic response.

But Scott caught my eye and grimaced just enough that I realized what I'd just said. "Actually, no," I quickly corrected, "we don't need to keep those sheets."

It was one of those silly things that sometimes happens at times of great emotion or great strain, when a person isn't thinking clearly, but the memory of that question and answer made me laugh heartily in the days ahead. Why on earth would I want to keep the sheets that my mother died on? When and where would we ever possibly use them again?

Instead, the funeral director used those pretty floral sheets, which my mother had loved, to wrap her body like a shroud. They carried her out on a something that resembled a hammock, and I finally stepped away from the door as they lifted her into the SUV-style hearse. We closed the door and I went to join my family in the living room.

Grief

*Plummeting down
into massive water deeper than the sky,
sinking fast, jagged fear in my lungs, unable to breathe,
unable even to gasp,
sinking, sinking in the violent peace
of drowning. No sight, no smell,
all silent. But tasting the bitter salty bile as it fills me.
Reaching out my arms, nothing to grasp,
but slowing to a spin, turning, dizzying with no senses,
no sense of above or below, no direction toward light.
Floating and spinning, knowing I'll drown
knowing I cannot survive here.
Panic and resignation together.
This consuming water holds me,
and instinctively I kick, just once,
and feel the lift
beginning to be taken toward the surface,
and for a moment I think relief is ahead.
Letting myself go,
not fighting the water, I rise and break
through the surface
only to be assaulted by wind and cold, weighty
waves over my head.
I gasp for air, but pounding water pushes me down
again and again, as I flail and fight.
I want to give up
but I taste the air now, sharp and fleeting, but there.
Wave after wave smashing and splashing
as my screams are filled with the heavy water,*

bouncing me under and up, under and up, under and up.
I let go
and feel the pull, the push, the current.
Suddenly I glimpse it—just a blink of sight,
the shoreline is see-sawing in the distant light
so far from where I am.
Closing my eyes again to the hammering surf,
I cannot swim, I cannot tread water
yet.
I surrender and sink and fight and float
until it's there again, in my sight, the shore.
Bobbing in the breakers, still feeling the wash of waves,
I am moving toward it.
Slowing, slowly moving,
so slow. But I see it more clearly, more steadily
and I'm facing the place where the water meets the sand.
My arms and legs know what to do, and
I'm struggling still in the siege of the water,
yet moving.
And the water begins to calm.
I feel myself drifting back, not controlling anything
just coasting toward the coast.
Rocking in the current.
And then I feel it,
my toe scrapes the solid sand
searching for a foothold
until I can begin to walk through the water.
The effort, the drag, still holding me back
making me stumble in slow motion side-stepping.
My gaze is fixed, but the shore is detached from me,
impossibly far.
The current now pushes and pulls, pushes
and pulls, shoving me and releasing me with each step
feeling the sand shift beneath my soles.
My shoulders and chest emerge,
the relentless liquid still hugging my waist.

*Step, step, step, my hips are freed and I begin
to feel shells and shapes beneath my feet,
scratching and smooth, and rough.
My knees emerge, now, and the watery sand holds my weight.
I walk cautiously as waves splash my back, still cold, still shocking,
and my self emerges
dripping the heartbreak
into the ankle-deep foam, soaked and heavy with water
I walk on.
But the dry sand looks foreign, and the ocean familiar,
so I wander along the edge
where the water meets the sand
with the spray in my face and the waves always lapping at my feet.
Lapping but not consuming, cold and surprising, but not
devouring.
And as the tides change, I alter my course to accommodate the danger
knowing I might drift out again into the ocean
but knowing, too,
I am strong.*

Chapter 9
Life Without My Mother

The sounds inside our house were the first things I noticed. The sounds had changed.

Despite feeling slightly dazed, I realized that we were all talking at regular volume, not speaking softly and worrying about anyone asleep somewhere else in the house. We were picking things up and setting them down without trying to be especially quiet. We were calling to each other from different rooms.

"Does anyone need something to drink?"

"Is there anyone else we have to call tonight?"

There were also sounds of crying and conversation, and occasionally the sound of a tiny bit of laughter, as we talked about some memories and funny stories. Our evenings hadn't resonated like that in a long time, not in this house where we lived with my mother. I perceived the change in our vibrations right away, as soon as my mother was gone.

My mother, Ellen, was gone.

But while we were moving around the house with a different sort of ease, I also felt acutely aware of my mother, as if her absence itself had substance. While I could no longer hear her voice out loud, I still heard her voice in my head and in my heart.

My sisters and I felt that she might be giving us signs already of her presence with us, her presence in spirit. That afternoon, I picked up a bookmark of hers from her bookshelf in the den, one that I'd seen her use frequently but that I'd never looked at closely, and the writing on the bookmark was a quote from St. Francis de Sales: "Make yourself familiar with the angels, and behold them frequently in spirit; for without being seen, they are present with you."

I read it and I wondered if my mother was going to be like an angel, perhaps a guardian angel for our family. The timing of picking up that bookmark seemed miraculous to me. The miracle is often in the timing. I've always believed that.

Miraculous things can often things can be explained away as coincidence or by scientific explanations, but I think that it's the timing that makes things miraculous.

I found that bookmark exactly when I needed to, and the wording had meaning to me. I'm sure it had been sitting in that same spot for weeks, but the *timing* of me noticing it made it feel like something divine.

On the day following my mother's passing, Scott and Zoe and I met my sister and nephew at a local restaurant for breakfast. They had chosen to stay at a hotel after their long, heartbreaking drive the night before, and I appreciated having the time overnight without houseguests, because I'd spent several hours during the night sitting in the recliner in the den, looking at the empty hospital bed.

It was a Friday morning, and the breakfast with them gave us all an opportunity to step outside the house, literally, and to clear our brains a little bit from the events and emotions of the preceding few days. I remember thinking that it felt dreamlike to be out in a restaurant, all of us together, knowing the still inconceivable truth that my mother had died.

After breakfast, we all went back to our house and my sisters and I made calls to everyone on my mother's calling list, two of us working from my house, and my eldest sister making calls from her own home several states away. We divided up the list and started making calls as soon as we could, and we checked in with each other after every few calls just to fill each other in on what people had said in response to the sad news.

Zoe and my nephew, as well as Scott, wandered around the house chatting about my mother and about other things too. Scott tried to clean up the house a bit. None of us really knew what to do with ourselves, but I appreciated the occupation of making calls and making arrangements.

I called the funeral director in Glenside and set up an appointment for the following Monday morning to meet and go over all the details of the arrangements, most of which he already had in his file from our pre-planning and pre-payment paperwork. But I'd have to go to the Funeral Home in person, because I'd need to drop off the clothing that my mother wanted to be wearing.

We arranged over the phone that the services would take place a week later, the following Friday and Saturday, and that timeframe gave my sisters and their families, as well as me, Scott, Abby and Zoe, enough time to make arrangements to travel to Pennsylvania. My sister and nephew headed back home later that day, and we said goodbye knowing that we'd be together again in a week.

The medical equipment company arrived that same day with a truck to take away my mother's supplies. They took out the hospital bed first, and I watched it go out the door with some melancholy. Then, they came back in for the unused commode, the unused oxygen tank, the unused oxygen concentrator, and the wheelchair that had been used only a handful of times. I was especially sad to see the shower chair go out the door, because it reminded me of how cheerful my mother became after the visits from her hospice aide.

She'd feel refreshed and somehow fortified with those showers and hairdos. And yet, I knew that I'd be getting some space back in my bathroom, since the chair would no longer be standing in there. Guilty relief, for sure.

The walker, and the jingle bells, belonged to us and were ours to keep. I took the jingle bells off the walker almost immediately, because I simply couldn't stand to hear them if anyone moved the walker. The sound was connected to my mother; the jingling bells had become my continual call, my persistent summons. I wrapped them in a small towel, to silence them, and I put them into a drawer.

I also removed the two signs from the windows in her bedroom and den, which had warned about oxygen on the premises for the past five months. She had forgotten that those signs were there, hidden behind the curtains, but I noticed them almost every time I left the house. The simple act of pulling the scotch tape off the window glass and taking those signs out of the windows was simultaneously freeing and painful for me.

I don't remember exactly how we spent the following day, which was a Saturday, but I'm sure that we were on the phone with friends and family members, and I was probably starting to make some notes, both mental notes and actual to-do lists, of what all of the next steps needed to be. I know that I'd written the obituary in advance, with my mother's oversight, so that was already done.

Similarly, she had left behind the complete instructions for her funeral, so I only had to remind each family member what their roles would be. My mother left photo albums for each of her daughters and grandchildren, so I also packed them up to be handed out when we gathered for the funeral.

On that Sunday, Zoe and I drove to Pennsylvania together. We planned to stay overnight with close friends so that Zoe and I could go to the funeral home on Monday morning. But in the meantime, we went to another funeral, the one for my friend's mother, who had died a few days before my mother. By some peculiar stroke of grace, I had been able to finish writing the eulogy for my friend to read at her mother's funeral just before my own mother had passed.

So, we went to that funeral on Sunday afternoon, and I sat there as if I was in a trance. Lucky for me, the format of that funeral was completely different from what I knew was coming later in the week for my own mother. So, I was able to think about my friend's mother and somehow separate it out from the overwhelming thoughts about my own mother.

I even stood and spoke a few words about my childhood memories of my friend's family when guests were invited to do that. I tried to compartmentalize my own loss, because I would have completely fallen apart if I had let myself think only about my own mother on that day. I'm not quite sure how I got through it, except for the support of my two friends who stayed with me and Zoe throughout, never leaving our side, making sure we were okay.

Afterwards, Zoe and I headed to the home of those two friends. We watched the Tony Awards that evening, which seemed bizarre, but wonderful, and had some cocktails. I thought about how much my mother loved Broadway musicals, but I also knew that she had stopped watching all awards shows many years earlier, partly because she objected to the low-cut gowns that many of the women wore, and specifically for the Tonys, she also didn't like any suggestive lyrics in her show tunes. But it was exactly the right distraction for us on that peculiar Sunday evening.

Zoe went with me to the funeral home first thing Monday. We sat with the funeral director in a little sort of living room, with arm chairs, loveseat and coffee table arranged together in the corner of a much larger room. He had all of our paperwork, so I just needed to review and sign off on everything. We handed over the hanger holding my mother's gown covered in plastic, and I smiled again remembering how pretty she had looked wearing that at my wedding.

We gave him the bag with her shoes and undergarments. We also gave him the photo of how she hoped they would make her look at the viewing, showing her hairstyle and very natural make-up. The photo was a good one. She was more than ten years younger and very happy. The photo had been taken by my father, and her smile showed that she was full of joy.

I told the funeral director that she had asked to be smiling, and to look the way she did in that photo. Even as I handed it to him, I knew that it was impossible. There was no way that she'd look so full of life because, obviously, she wasn't.

The days between that funeral home appointment and the actual funeral passed by quickly because I was so busy, and yet it was as if I was aware of every single second passing, like every one of my senses were heightened. Scott had taken those days off from work and his support was invaluable to me. But I remember witnessing his pain too, one morning when we were both in the kitchen getting our breakfast.

He had picked up a banana, and without thinking, he broke it in half and then turned toward the table with my mother's half of his banana in his outstretched hand, before he realized that her seat was empty. He silently bent at the waist, so that he was literally facing the floor, making no sound at all, until I heard his choked sob burst out of him in one unforgettable noise.

Abby arrived from Salt Lake City but Alan couldn't come with her due to his work and school commitments. It felt like a balm to have her with us because she didn't like being so far away during her grandmother's decline. She had wanted to come sooner, but we didn't know what to expect. Still, her hugs felt like a connection that had been missing. I know that she and Zoe helped to hold each other up too. I felt overwhelming gratitude for my daughters that week.

We made hotel reservations for the upcoming weekend in Pennsylvania. We debated about staying in the area for a few nights, because the funeral home was just a few blocks from the house in Glenside that we'd moved out of several months earlier. But we decided to book our hotel for only one night, because I knew that I wouldn't want to socialize or get caught up in other activities. I wanted to give my mother her farewell and get out of there quickly.

I sensed, rather than knew, that I was going to have some rough days and weeks ahead. I was starting to realize that I had never fully grieved for my father, because I so quickly became my mother's on-site support person. I had to rise to that role immediately when he passed, and now that she was gone, I was suddenly and ferociously feeling his loss too.

But during that week before the funeral, I was able to keep busy and keep focused on practical plans, so I was able to hold myself together. I could, however, feel the waves of grief building up.

During that week, I also felt a pressing need to reach out to a special friend Kathleen, because I hadn't spoken with her in a few years. She was the daughter of my mother's dear friend, my Aunt Loretta, and we had grown up together. But complications of adulthood had come between us a few years earlier, and our once inseparable friendship had disintegrated.

I debated about whether or not to call Kathleen and her brother to share the news of my mother's death, because I wasn't sure if she'd want to hear from me.

I settled on sending a text message. To my relief, she responded quickly, and we began a text conversation. I felt immediately hopeful that we might be able to sort through our difficulties eventually, and maybe I'd have my friend back. I felt like my mother would have been pleased with this.

I also used those days before the funeral to start figuring out what I'd need to do as the executor of my mother's will. My mother had enjoyed using the word *executrix* to describe me, but I was glad to learn that the official language had become less gender specific since her days working in the legal field. I was told that when I had the death certificates, I would need to go to the courthouse in Baltimore County to register her will.

That would begin the process that I was dreading. I was glad that I didn't have to do anything immediately, because I wanted to get through the funeral first.

The four of us drove to Pennsylvania together. It was a normal drive, except that I had a horrible feeling of a lump in my throat that I couldn't get rid of. We checked into our hotel and then we met my sisters and their families for lunch. It felt a bit like a family reunion, with a lot of laughter, but there was also a sense that any of us might burst into tears at any moment.

My tears were just below the surface through the whole meal. I wanted to shake someone, anyone, maybe a stranger at the next table, and cry out, *"Don't you know that my mother has died?"* It didn't feel right to me to act normally.

After lunch, we went back to our hotels and got changed into funeral clothes for the viewing that evening. My mother had specified that she wanted an open casket. We all met again at the funeral home in Glenside. I can still picture exactly what the steps looked like as we walked from the parking lot into the funeral home, and I can see the details of the little hallway leading to the larger room where we'd find my mother lying in her casket.

I think that I was the first one who walked into the room, with my sisters very close by me, and we turned a corner to see my mother's body. As I knew she'd be, she was wearing the turquoise gown from my wedding and she was holding the little bouquet of five roses, three pink and two white, as she'd requested. She was surrounded by lovely floral arrangements, from her own friends, from cousins, from friends and in-laws of myself and my sisters, and even one from the friend who I had recently reconnected with and her brother.

But my mother didn't look like herself.

Her face was different, as, of course, it had to be. The funeral make-up looked foreign on her skin, as she rarely wore any foundation at all. The lipstick seemed too dark, too precise, and her hair was just a shade darker than it should have been. I could see that they had used the photo as a guide, but I think that it wasn't a realistic goal. She didn't look young and happy; she looked unnatural to me. It broke my heart.

It wasn't until later that I realized that I had simply wanted her to look *alive*. Even though I was completely familiar with the mortuary process, and I should have known what to expect, it was different when I was looking at my own mother. I had wanted her to look like she was sleeping. But she didn't. She didn't look soft any more. Seeing her like that, as a dead woman dressed for burial, I felt the full impact of the finality of her earthly life.

Still, the viewing was actually quite beautiful. We started out standing in a receiving line so that guests could walk along and greet everyone in the family, but we quickly fell out of that formation. My sisters and I couldn't resist walking forward to greet and hug relatives that we hadn't seen for years and old friends. I tried to stand in the place where the funeral director had wanted us to be, but when I saw one of my best friends from childhood, who had lived right up the street from me, I couldn't contain myself.

I had to rush over to greet her. It was not at all a somber event. Eventually, there was no receiving line at all and we all just walked around from group to group catching up and reminiscing. People laughed and joked, and we heard quite a few stories about my mother, and about my father too. If we had had beverages, it might have seemed like a cocktail party atmosphere.

I think that my mother would have liked that jovial gathering. We heard people express gratitude to my mother for being warm and loving toward them, and those stories brought true comfort for our loss.

Every now and then, I glanced over at the casket, at my mother's body lying there, and a few times I walked over and stood by her for a moment. I didn't want to forget that she was with us. I didn't want to turn my back on her. And in those moments, I felt myself starting to drown in the grief again, as if I could barely swallow, barely breathe.

It wasn't registering fully for me at that point, but I felt that my world had changed. The viewing felt like an occasion, and on every other occasion when my mother had been with me, I had spent my time trying to address her needs.

Was she hungry? Was she cold? Was she comfortable? Did she get to talk to everyone? But on that evening, she didn't need anything anymore.

I was just looking at her, not really doing anything for her, and that was a seismic shift. This was the first time in my fifty-two years of life that I was living without my mother.

The funeral mass the following morning was exactly as my mother had wanted. It was a beautiful sunny day and we gathered early at the church for one last private family viewing before the funeral director closed the casket for the final time. We all had a few moments, and I touched her hand, as she was still clutching those five flowers, and I told her that I loved her. Just before they lowered that lid, I whispered to her, "Sleep tight, Mommy."

Once the casket was closed, guests started to arrive for the funeral mass, and this time we did stay in an orderly receiving line at the front of the church by the casket. My mother's priest friend was the officiant for the mass. I was deeply touched at how many people from my own spiritual community at Abington Friends Meeting showed up for the funeral. We had far more Quakers than Catholics in the church that day.

I felt that I was being supported by these Friends and held in the Light for strength that day. It felt especially meaningful to me to have Friends there, because I was acutely aware of being the non-Catholic daughter, especially while in the church.

The mass seemed much more formal and final to me than the viewing had felt. We were seated in the church pews and we followed the order of the mass, and all of the family members, including her dear friend, the Sister of Mercy, participated as my mother had wanted. The music and the program were exactly as she had planned, although we added some beautiful photo collages that my middle sister put together, and my eldest sister's husband read a eulogy that we all had contributed to.

My sister had wanted to read it herself but it seemed easier for her husband to do it. As he read it, and he joked that he was my mother's favorite, I smiled to myself realizing that my mother had an extraordinary gift of making everyone feel special, like each one was her favorite. Everyone who attended the funeral also had an opportunity to speak messages about my mother, and we again heard some lovely remembrances, and some funny stories too.

We buried my mother in the same grave as my father at a Catholic cemetery near Glenside. We drove in our own cars, following the hearse, and we parked our cars in a line along the curb in the same area where I'd helped my mother out of my car so often when I'd taken her to visit my father's grave. It felt strange that she wasn't with me as we got out of the car and started walking along that familiar stretch of grass.

As my mother had requested, we had a bagpiper playing *Danny Boy*, her favorite song, as the casket was carried to the grave. Sadly, I don't think I heard it at all. I knew that the bagpipes were playing but the song escaped me as I watched the pallbearers slowing walking with the casket that held my mother's body. I wanted so badly to be holding her arm again, guiding her so that she wouldn't fall, as we walked together.

But this time, the pallbearers were carrying her to her final resting place, with Zoe and my niece walking in procession with them. My mother no longer needed to lean on me and I only had to walk behind.

Her priest friend offered some blessings at the graveside, and my sisters and I sat in folding chairs while many of our friends and family stood behind and around us. There was a bright green mat that looked like artificial grass going right up to the open grave, where the casket rested on the lowering equipment. I stared at the casket knowing that my mother's body was inside, and I thought about never touching her again.

I thought about her hands, how I used to love to look at them and hold them. I thought about brushing her hair, and about sitting on her bedside with my arm around her frail shoulders, gently hugging her. And I remembered how she'd smile at me.

As is the custom with Catholic cemeteries, we left the graveside before the casket was lowered. As the guests walked back to their cars, several people hugged me and spoke with me, but I kept feeling the pull of the casket behind me. I stopped walking a few times, while Scott and my daughters waited patiently, and I finally had to go back to the casket one last time by myself, after everyone else had walked away.

I knew that I had to say one last thing to her before they lowered her body into the ground. I reached out my hand and touched the casket, and I just kept my hand there for a few moments.

"Sleep tight, my good friend," I whispered to her.

We went to a German restaurant for a buffet luncheon after the burial, and I was glad to see how many friends joined us. I enjoyed the relaxed ambience, with guests walking around and chatting, but I was starting to feel exhausted too, and just wanted to get home. After we said goodbye to my sisters and the whole family, Scott and I got back into the car with Abby and Zoe and headed south, back to Maryland.

As we usually do after events, we reviewed everything that had happened over the previous few days. We talked all through the car ride about seeing old friends and about how it felt to be back in our beloved Glenside, but for such a sad occasion. At a few points in the conversation, I let myself just look out the window and listen to the voices around me. It all felt like it was happening outside of me, like these days had been unreal.

When we got back to our home, it felt different too. It felt the way our home in Glenside had felt, before we moved and lived with my mother. It felt relaxed and I felt like I could finally fully exhale, but it also felt like something, or some*one*, was missing. During the next few weeks and months, as summertime warmed and lit our home, I waded through my grief and started to appreciate that we had our summer to ourselves as a family.

It felt more free and calm because I wasn't caring for my mother anymore, and I was grateful for that. That gratitude, along with my huge relief that things had never gotten so bad with my mother's care that I couldn't handle her at home, helped me get through the early stages of loss.

As we returned home on the day of the funeral, it hit me almost as soon as we walked in the door. The absence of my mother in this house where she had been with us almost every day since we moved in was palpable. The stress and tension were gone, but so was her existence. I suddenly realized as I walked through the house, *I don't have parents any more.*

Strangely, I think that immediately after my mother's funeral, I felt the loss of my father more than the loss of her. It had certainly been building up for ten years, as I'd been supporting my mother and trying to stay strong for her. My memories of him came flooding back, and I could picture him physically as if he was right next to me.

I heard his laughter in my memory and I remembered his gruffness and his kindness. I think that maybe he was really with me quite vividly in spirit during those days, while my mother was still transitioning to the other side. I felt like he was keeping me company. But I felt the physical, earthly loss of him immensely.

And there were many, many times when I'd sit alone in my mother's bedroom, just quietly sitting on her bed not doing anything except thinking about her and crying. Sometimes, I'd speak to her out loud, and I'd also speak to her silently at times, knowing that she could probably connect with me in a different, spiritual way since passing. But that spiritual presence didn't take away the grief. It didn't take away the awareness that I'd never hold her hand again.

I stayed extremely busy in the following months sorting through my mother's things, both as executor of her will and as the person who had to clean out her bedroom and den. I had no idea what I was in for, because when my father died, my mother and I handled most of this stuff together. This time, it all fell to me.

The official copies of her death certificate eventually arrived, and I was struck by the formality of this document that summed up in so few words all that had happened on the evening that my mother died. Just the facts. *Time of death*: 2150. *Immediate Cause*: Congestive Heart Failure. *Date of Death, Location of Death. Marital Status, Decedent's Education, Father's Name, Mother's Name.* And then I saw the box asking for *Informant's Name,* and there was my own name.

It surprised me to see my name, but I sort of liked that connection, that I was part of her permanent record. I was right there on the certificate, part of the cold and succinct wording. *Relationship*: Daughter.

I made my appointments and went to the Baltimore County courthouse, to a Maryland accountant, and to a branch of her bank. The paperwork seemed endless during the following weeks, which stretched into months of repeat trips to the courthouse and the bank and the accountant. I took days off from work because I had so many phone calls to make to follow up on legalities of her bank accounts, her insurance policies and her will, and to cancel Social Security, health insurance, even magazine subscriptions.

It was endless. I had two drawers in her dresser that were completely filled with her paperwork. There were many times that I was in tears because I was simply overwhelmed with all that needed to be done. And yet, having these tasks kept me occupied and helped with the grief.

Way before she died, my mother prepared a long list, several pages in fact, of all of her personal assets and how they should be distributed. She had started this list before my father died. There were separate pages for me and for each of my sisters. She specified exactly who should get what. During her lifetime, she had started to pre-enforce her wishes by using permanent markers to actually write our names onto many of her belongings.

It was an unfortunate idea but she stood by it. For many years, if someone lifted up a figurine at my parents' house, they'd find bold black letters with my name or one of my sister's names indicating who would eventually receive this item. Everything was labelled. Record albums, knickknacks, wall hangings.

In some cases, it probably decreased the value of the particular items to have permanent marker on them, and I also tried to tell her so many times that this was not a good idea because it also meant that our names would be on those items whenever we might pass them on to our own children, or if we wanted to swap with each other. But she was relentless with her markers.

Before we moved to Maryland, she used that lengthy assets list as she cleaned out her apartment. Some of the items had already been given to each of us over the years, so the list had some items crossed-out, but as she prepared for her final move, she asked each of us to claim and take away the remaining items from our lists. Each of my sisters visited and filled their vehicles with everything that they wanted, and I brought my things to my house as we were packing too.

Admittedly, there was some swapping of items, and there were several things that none of us really wanted. My mother was really surprised at some of the things that were refused, because she had always assumed that we'd want everything. So, she brought a bit more with her to Maryland than she'd hoped, but we sorted through some of it together as we unpacked in the new house. Still, it made my job far easier after she died, knowing that my sisters had already taken everything that they wanted.

My emotions were in high gear as I set about sorting the rest of her things. For some reason, possibly just to feel a sense of normality again, I felt some urgency in redecorating the den. Yet, at the same time, I barely wanted to touch or change anything in her bedroom. The den was easier.

We already knew that neither of my sisters wanted any of the furniture that had been in the den, so I donated my mother's two old recliners, her two large bookshelves and her sideboard to families in need. It was as if I couldn't wait to see those furnishings go out the door. It gave me a sense of cleaning out the negativity, getting a fresh start, and I desperately wanted to claim that space in the den for happier times.

I found a small sectional sofa that exactly fit the room, so no additional furniture was needed. The space was suddenly much more open and felt free from clutter. I put our own books onto the built-in bookshelf, but I kept one shelf of my mother's books in place, exactly as she had them. I also left in place, displayed next to our fireplace, my father's Irish walking stick, which I had given to him, and my mother's old manual typewriter, on which I first started to write poetry as an adolescent.

So, it was only a few weeks until the den felt better to me, as if I was able to leave behind the patient-caregiver space, and reclaim it as a special room where my mother made her final transition into death, but where the family could gather with a sense of lightness.

Her bedroom, however, felt much more precious and delicate to me. I already knew that I'd likely want to eventually use that room as an office, but I felt no urgency at all in cleaning it out. Sorting the bedroom was a much more gradual process than the den, and I actually had to plan and schedule time for myself to clean out her things, because I kept procrastinating. I just didn't want to do it. The thought of carrying empty trash bags into her bedroom expecting to fill them with her belongings made me literally tremble at times.

I also knew that after such a long and emotional journey together with my mother, I needed to clean out her things by myself. It felt like I owed it to her to sort through everything she left behind, just me alone in her room, although I dreaded making the inevitable decisions, over and over, on which items to throw away.

The sorting process brought me to some interesting and amusing discoveries. I found many handbags, or pocketbooks, as she called them, all squished into Rubbermaid containers in the bottom of her closet. She had pocketbooks in bright colors as well as black, white and neutral beiges. Most were fake leather and all of them had many pockets and zippered compartments. I had never seen her use most of them.

I was already aware that my mother had a lot of very similar shirts, because I'd helped her to hang up a full row, at least two feet long in her closet, of just those pale colored polo shirts. Before she became sick, she wore a similar shirt every day. She had plenty of other shirts too, but as I cleaned out her bedroom, I started to find more and more of the similar shirts hidden behind other things in the dresser and bureau drawers and in the containers.

I laughed so hard every time I found another bunch of them, that I actually counted them. She had sixty-two short sleeved polo shirts, all stashed in various places in her bedroom. It was hilarious, until it made me sad to realize that at some point, long before she moved in with us, she had ordered all of those shirts from catalogues, either forgetting that she already owned so many of them, or, as I suspect was true, wanting to make sure that she had enough back-up shirts in case any of them got ripped or stained.

This was a woman who had kept three half gallons of milk in her refrigerator at all times, just so that she'd be prepared and never run out; she liked having back-ups. We donated the polo shirts to a local Goodwill, and I couldn't help thinking that if there was some organized group in the area, like a marching band, they could purchase all the shirts as uniforms.

Cleaning out her last few personal belongings was the longest process of all. There are still a few drawers that I may never empty out because it's too painful for me to get rid of the precious items that she treasured. Most of them are practically useless to me, except for the fact that they were so meaningful to her. Her hand-held mirror that my father had given to her, her handkerchiefs, her address book, her paper calendar from the months before she died where she scribbled notes in every square, most appearing as gibberish to me now.

These items sit in her dresser drawers still. I've consolidated her things into just a few drawers and I use the remaining drawers for my office supplies, because I've changed her bedroom into the place where I work. I feel her presence in this room more than anywhere else. She slept here, she prayed here, she thought and dreamed and wished here. And my desk chair sits in approximately the same place where she and I used to sit on the edge of her bed, me with my arm around her tiny shoulders, talking together before bedtime.

She is with me. I know this for sure.

Throwing It All Away

Well, not everything
but many things, the belongings she left behind
that none of us wanted
to keep. Her treasures
become another person's trash?
A painful reversal for me,
as I sort through the row of hangers with tiny-print polo shirts,
boxes and boxes of shoes, some the same pairs
in varying levels of being worn out. All in the closet
unclaimed.
Maybe donations to Goodwill,
maybe a way to recycle.
Each chipped knickknack remembers her
and every garment holds her scent.
Her books with yellowing pages, crumbling covers,
her green plastic curlers,
and hair nets and nail files,
and five pairs of scissors in her dresser drawer,
her pale shades of Cover Girl lipstick rarely worn,
all wait like sentinels watching for her return.
But she will disappoint them
and I'll put them in a bag.
I start and I stop, needing to breathe, fighting back tears
knowing that this chore will wait
and wait
for me to see and touch each piece,
some that I recognize, some that make me laugh out loud
wondering when she acquired that,
why she saved this.

I sort and smile and cry,
but it feels like a search.
If I only knew what I'm looking for.
What am I trying to find in these drawers and closets,
what did she possess that I need now?
Maybe I'll know when I see it.

Chapter 10
My Journey

My appetite may be the thing that best defines me.

And I'm not talking about food. Well, not *only* about food, because concerns about my weight have shaped me (pun intended) throughout my life. I'm talking about an appetite that touches every aspect of life, a craving for more. It's an overarching need for more information, for more clarity, for more understanding—and this has led me to continue down the path I've been on since childhood.

That desire for deeper connections eventually brought me to spirit mediumship, a skill that I hadn't expected to cultivate. But during my time as a caregiver for my mother, I started to notice that all of my life experiences had brought me to the threshold of discovering even more possibilities.

When I was little, I played by myself a lot. My main play space was our basement, where I'd stay for hours and hours, or else I'd be playing alone in my bedroom. I even sat on our front steps by myself, reading or daydreaming, sitting there long enough that the little boy across the street walked over to ask me if I was okay. He suggested some good shows that were on TV, but I told him I was fine. I enjoyed being alone. I liked feeling solitary.

When I played alone, the games were all mine. I could decide what to have happen in my imaginary adventures while I played dress-ups, or what the daily activities of my dolls would be. I could choose to spend time coloring, or playing with toys, or listening to music. My options were wide open. Entertaining myself like that forced me to think. It was an environment where I was figuring things out independently.

I didn't have to follow anyone else's rules when I played alone, and I had time to explore and be creative. All of this alone time had an effect on who I became as an adult.

In college, I had a button with the words *Question Authority*, and I wore it proudly on my denim jacket all the time. I also had a button that said *Shut Up and Dance*. Those seemed like two opposing points of view, but I interpreted the second one to be a reminder to myself, saying *'Stop complaining and start enjoying life!'* Both of those buttons had messages that I carried into my adulthood.

In those formative years, I wanted to be a person who could find out things for myself, make my own choices, and also take every opportunity to enjoy the beauty of the world around me.

My parents, especially my mother, taught me about Catholicism, and in childhood, I loved that tradition and the community I found within the religion. I learned the rituals and prayers and I absorbed the charm and the reassurance from Catholic practices. From my mother, I learned to value my relationship with God and to prioritize my spiritual life.

Mostly, I knew that it pleased my parents for me to believe what they believed. But I was by nature, and probably by nurture too, a questioning person. I didn't want to follow anyone else's rules unless they made sense to me and brought me inner joy. So, I think it was inevitable that I'd become a person who explored varying spiritual practices. I think that the independence I'd learned in childhood led to a sense of longing in me, and that sense of longing led me to my religious studies.

When I decided to choose a different direction for my life and leave the Catholic Church, it was truly heart wrenching for me. But it wasn't a choice that came easily or quickly. Although, my ultimate choice did occur when I was raising my children, I had been on a journey of exploration for many years before that. Because of that journey, I came to my decision about Catholicism with a lot of clarity about my own beliefs. I hadn't found what I needed within my parents' religion, and I was drawn to spiritual practices that were different from my own.

It wasn't just practices and traditions that fascinated me. I also had an awareness of spirits around me, around all of us. Actually, my mother taught me about spirits too. She had often talked about our family members who had passed, and she told me that she talked to them out loud, sometimes while going about her daily business, folding laundry, dusting the living room. All the time, she was aware of spirits around her.

So, I think I inherited my interest in spirits from the descriptions she shared. Then, when we were together at the end of her life, it was obvious that she continued to recognize the spirits around us at that point too.

As I was caring for my mother, my awareness of all things supernatural increased.

Perhaps it was because I was spending all of my time so closely connected with her as she was close to her own death, but it seemed like my extrasensory perception was heightened. I sensed the presence of my father frequently. I could sometimes hear him as if he was whispering to me. He encouraged me to stay strong and he thanked me for keeping my promise to take care of my mother after he died.

I also felt my Oma with me. I had the impression that she was giving me strength and reminding me to stand up for myself when my mother's more judgmental personality annoyed me. My Opa was also with me, holding my hand with his gentle support and good humor. I saw all of them as shadows at times, moving about our house. I felt that all of them existed just beyond an invisible veil, and that they were just a whisper away from me.

Sometimes, when I'd approach my mother's bedroom in the early morning, I'd hear her talking. When I'd ask her who she was talking to, she'd tell me that she was talking with my father, or with her parents. There was one night that was especially bad for my mother, with pain and breathing distress that the medication didn't seem to resolve, and she spent most of that night, as I sat by her side, speaking in German to her own mother.

Her gaze was fixed, as if she was looking directly at my grandmother while she spoke, and she paused to listen to answers that I couldn't hear. I have no doubt that my Oma was there with her, with us.

I received a couple of spirit readings during the time that my mother lived with us, using Zoom or Skype to meet with spirit mediums online. I scheduled those readings because I was hoping to connect with my loved ones in spirit, and I was worried that all of the caregiving pressures I was feeling might be disrupting my own direct connection. In the readings, I was assured that my mother would not need to go into a nursing home, and that I'd be able to handle her care at home until the end.

The readings told me that I wasn't alone, and that I could call on friends in spirit when I needed their extra support. Often, when I'd silently pray and ask for that support, I'd feel chills wash over me, as if I was being given physical confirmation of their presence.

I often found myself asking for grace, for the patience and strength to continue as a caregiver, and I prayed to God, the divine Creator, the Great Spirit. There are many names for that force of love in our Universe. Since a very early age, I referred to Jesus in my prayers as *Friend*. It's not lost on me that as a Quaker, I'm part of the Religious Society of Friends. It seemed inevitable, really.

The experience of sensing spirits around me has not seemed to be in contrast with my Quaker values. In Quakerism, the belief in Continuing Revelation means that every person is capable of experiencing the divine directly and personally, without needing clergy or others to bring forth the divine Spirit. So, it seems to me that if we can personally connect with the divine, we might also be able to connect with our families and friends in spirit.

However, this is not specifically stated anywhere in Quaker faith and practice, so I'm only referring to my own experience. I've enjoyed the open-mindedness of Quakerism.

Quakerism appeals to me in other ways as well. The awareness of the Light within all people, a Light that defies explanation, speaks to me. In my Quaker community, as with many of my family and friends, we come together to help each other grow and heal and move toward enlightenment. There's a sort of magic that isn't easy to define when a group of people gather together with the expectation of being moved by the Spirit.

Yet, I know that the magical feeling that comes with deep spiritual experiences can happen anywhere. When I was living in Washington State in my early twenties, I remember walking up into the hills and feeling that I wasn't alone. I felt as if I was in the presence of other beings, even though I couldn't see them.

I wished that I knew how to communicate with them, although I already had a sense that they could give me signs to help guide me through my own life. The feeling that spirits were around me continued to grow, and I realized that at times I felt like the spirits were actually trying to reach out to me, to communicate.

And I am fully aware of how crazy that might seem to some people.

I realize that many people are skeptical about this sort of thing. I was a sceptic about spirit readings myself until I had some readings that seemed undeniably precise and accurate. My own doubts led me to learn about mediumship, to try to understand how it happens that some people seem to be able to connect with spirits. I opened my mind enough to admit possibilities, to acknowledge that maybe there's more to this world than we can see and hear and touch with our ordinary senses.

Honestly, it wasn't much of a stretch for me, and I never really thought that any of this metaphysical stuff was crazy, because I'd been experiencing it for years without even trying.

The first time I felt the real presence of a spirit, it was Saint Therese. Yes, the Catholic saint, the one nicknamed *The Little Flower*. I had read books about her because I was interested in her from an early age. I loved the idea that she said during her lifetime that she was going to spend eternity showering people with roses. I also understood that her *shower of roses* promise was meant to be a metaphor, meaning that she was going to help people overcome difficulties.

To my dismay, I later realized that some people had a very different impression of that promise. I once went with a friend to visit the property of a religious order where, on the feast day of Saint Therese, a helicopter flew overhead with a guy tossing roses down to the crowd gathered below. It had been advertised as *The Shower of Roses*, but we really hadn't expected such a literal interpretation.

It felt surreal as people jostled and pushed each other trying to catch a rose as the flowers fell through the gusty wind created by the loud helicopter. My friend and I stood there laughing, but I did manage to pick up a rose from the ground after the initial stampede had settled down, and miraculously, my rose wasn't crushed. Even more amazingly, that bizarre experience didn't damper my interest in Saint Therese. It was quite obvious that she had become a pop-culture saint, but I still admired the simplicity of her life, and I had my own direct experience with her.

I saw her when I was a young adult, standing in the corner of my bedroom as clear as day. There was a glow around her, as if light was emanating from her, and she was standing there life-size, smiling at me. She held a bouquet of roses in one hand, and her other hand was resting over her heart. I saw her in full color, and the nun's habit she was wearing was a bright blue and the roses were dark pink, appearing as if the colors were intensified and otherworldly.

I hadn't gone to sleep yet but my room was dark. I had been lying on my bed praying and thinking about my life and some important decisions ahead, and I just turned my head and saw her. She didn't move, and I was able to stare at her for a few moments before the image began to fade. And within a few moments,

I couldn't see her any longer, but I felt that presence with me as a source of comfort and protection.

I wasn't frightened about seeing a person standing in my bedroom because the presence had such a peaceful feeling about it. I also didn't question it, ever. I have no doubt in my mind that I saw Saint Therese standing in my room, and I know how goofy that seems. I really do. I didn't tell anyone about it until years later. But the experience did leave me wondering why I saw her, and what this meant. I knew with certainty that it wasn't a dream.

The second time I felt the real physical presence of a spirit, it was my father-in-law, a man that I'd never met. Scott and I had been married for over a year, and we were open to having a baby. On this particular night, I woke up from a sound sleep in the wee hours of morning and couldn't fall back to sleep. As I was lying in bed wide awake, I realized that my period might be a couple of weeks late, but I wasn't certain.

I wanted to get up and count the days on my calendar. I didn't want to wake Scott, so I left the bedroom and went to the kitchen to turn on a light and to figure out whether or not I was late. As soon as I looked at the calendar, I knew that I was indeed about two weeks late, and I excitedly started to wonder if it might be possible that I was pregnant. I turned off the lights again but instead of returning to bed, I went into our living room and sat on the sofa.

I was sitting with both feet on the floor, my back straight, and my hands in my lap, much like the position I use to meditate. I was tingling all over with the knowledge that I might be having a baby, so I'm sure my inner vibration was very high, and I was receptive to anything that the Universe would bring to me. Within a moment, I felt the presence. I knew instantly who it was and why he was there.

I turned my head slightly to my left, where we had a loveseat, and through the darkness I could feel Scott's father sitting there on that loveseat. I saw him almost as a shadow within the dark room. I felt him there and I knew that he was sitting with me because I was carrying his grandchild, and he was escorting this child into the physical world.

I knew with certainty at that moment that I was pregnant, even though it was so early. I sat there for over an hour, with my eyes open, aware that he was also sitting there with me in the living room. I looked over at him quite often, and he just smiled. We were both silent, in awe of the miracle that was happening for me and Scott.

I got a pregnancy test that morning after Scott left for work. Actually, I bought two tests, because I knew that I'd want to double-check. Both tests were positive and we eventually had Abby, whose first and middle names were chosen in honor of both her grandfather and Saint Therese.

Those types of spirit encounters continued for me. I once walked into the Quaker meetinghouse, on a day when it was empty, and I felt and saw in my mind's eye a man and a boy seated on a bench. Even though I didn't see them with my physical eyesight, I knew exactly what they were wearing and felt their presence as clearly as if they might walk over to me and start talking. But they stayed on that bench, appearing to be in silent worship, as Quakers of old would be.

So, my appetite for more information continued to expand and I took steps to study and learn as much as I could. I took several classes exploring spiritual practices that would be new to me. One was a Shamanic Journey class, and we met at the home of my teacher, a woman who trained in Guatemala to become a shaman. The class started as a larger group, but it eventually, over a couple of years, became just me and my meditation partner, along with the shaman.

She would drum for us and we would practice what she had guided us to do—to travel through mediation to the *Lower World* and the *Upper World*. In those meditative journeys, we learned to find our Power Animals, and mine was a fox. At first, I thought that this was a mistake, and that it happened because my name is Fox, but it was apparent to the shaman that I'm drawn to foxes and fox symbolism, even to the name Fox.

It made perfect sense to me. We also worked with our partners to find and identify our Spirit Guides, and not surprising to me, one of mine was Saint Therese.

I loved learning through the guidance of the shaman, and I felt my imagination exploding with ideas and clarity. My worldview shifted during those evenings and I began to see interconnectedness among all things. In several of the journeys, I felt the presence of Scott's first wife. She also came through for my mediation partner.

Sometimes, I'd have to check with Scott afterward to validate some of the things we experienced pertaining to her. He was skeptical but he indulged me. He was able to confirm what was coming through.

One specific thing was that Scott's first wife came through as feeling tied to our house, the house where Scott and I lived and where she had died. She wanted me to rid the house of something unpleasant that was keeping her connected there. Through several guided meditations, with the shaman's help, we figured out that it was the pole that had once held her IV fluids and medications, which had been left behind by the home healthcare team after she had died.

Scott had put it into the basement and it eventually became one of those things that you look at all the time without really seeing it. Eventually, it had been rolled to a side of the basement and Scott had random things hanging on it, as if it was just another hook on the wall. I had never even questioned why we had it, until this strange item became so pronounced in the meditations.

I felt that I was being asked to do something specific, so I went home and asked Scott if we could please get rid of the IV pole. Although, he was bewildered, even after I explained the shamanic journey experience I'd had, he went along with my request and got rid of it. The following week, when I went for the next class, his former wife again came through with the same request, that I get rid of the IV pole that was connecting her to that house in an unpleasant way.

I insisted that it was already gone but the messages continued without changing. The shaman suggested that I double-check that the pole was truly gone. So, when I got home, I asked Scott, "You did get rid of that IV pole, right?" He shrugged and said that he thought it might be useful someday, so he'd just pushed it into the corner by our hot water heater, where I couldn't really see it. I asked him to please get rid of it completely, and this time, he obliged.

The following week, his former wife came through for both me and my mediation partner, and she had a lightness and happiness that we hadn't felt in previous journeys. In our mediations, she said that she was able to move on and be only a happy and peaceful presence from now on, no longer feeling the sadness. She was able to let go and move forward. It felt as though she was thanking me.

In those same Shamanic Journey classes, we did an exercise to try to determine our purpose, our life's work. We did a guided meditation as the shaman drummed for us, and my message came to me quite clearly. The question had been: *What is my life's purpose?* And the response I received was: *To help people die.* I've thought about that often over the years.

At first, I thought that I was going to continue to work in hospice care, but later, I thought it might mean something on a more personal level. I had already been at my grandfather's side when he died, and then a few years after that shamanic journey, I was with my father when he died. Maybe I was somehow helping them to cross over.

Obviously, I wondered the same thing again when my mother received her terminal diagnosis and then moved in with us. I figured that this must be my role, my purpose, to be with people at their time of passing. Maybe it was my purpose to walk her up those stairs.

When I think back on the months that I was my mother's full time caregiver, I'm sometimes amazed that I survived. I'd had the darkest of thoughts, and I felt hopeless at times, doubting my ability to continue caring for her, and believing that the situation might drag on for years, with me longing for my privacy and wanting my own life routine to be returned to me.

I know what pulled me through. I know it for sure. I had the unending support of my family, but I also had something supernatural going on around me. I survived those difficult months with my sanity intact because I believed that I wasn't alone. I believed that help and support was not only coming from the people around me, but also from friends and family in spirit who were with me on another level.

Again, I know that this may seem completely unbelievable to some people.

When I felt myself getting overwhelmed and slipping, my spirit guides gave me signs that were just enough to calm me and give me renewed strength. I'd hear the perfect words at the perfect time, or something would catch my eye that brought me comfort or made me laugh.

Those little signs pulled me out of my worst thoughts. I felt that spirits were all around me, nudging me to pay attention. My mother spoke to them. I knew this and believed it, because it wasn't a new experience for me. In my opinion, it never seemed crazy. I've always accepted the idea that there must be more to our world than what we experience in our physical lives.

So, my journey with metaphysical spirituality began long before I became my mother's caregiver. But I learned some important things during the time I was taking care of her, and also in the time since her death. Something about the raw emotion and anxiety I felt while caring for my mother brought more of those beliefs to the surface for me.

When I was young, my mother used to come into my room and sit on the side of my bed after any loud fights in our house. I always knew that eventually she'd come in and sit with me for a little while to make sure I was okay. I was glad she did, because when voices were so loud and my family was yelling and struggling with each other, or when someone was being hit, I would notice my own hands trembling as I held onto my favorite rag doll, Suzy, as I waited there on my bed.

I just wanted the fighting to end. When my mother would finally come in, I'd talk to her about my fears and my wishes. She often responded by telling me she wished the same, for the fighting and conflicts to end. She went on to say that maybe I had the power to heal things for my family.

She told me, from a very young age, that I was a good writer and that my stories and poems might have just what it takes to change people's perspectives. She gave me an assignment, of sorts, to try to use my writing to heal any pain that I observed in our family, but I think she gave me more credit than I deserved. I tried to do what she asked, and I wrote story after story, poem after poem, during my elementary school and junior high years, some of them even with titles like *Saving Story* and *The Point of No Return*.

I wanted the readers to know instantly that what they were about to read would turn things around, like a figurative knock-on-the-head, getting them to see reason or to change their ways. My stories would save them. I had an unquenchable desire to do something grand that would fix everything.

Predictably, none of those stories or poems ever did anything like that. When I'd shared them with my family, sometimes even reading them out loud, I'd be told that they were very good. But the family dynamics didn't change. And when things did eventually get better, it wasn't at all due to anything I'd written.

I've often thought that part of my lifelong struggle with my weight has been a remnant of feeling like I wasn't able to succeed at saving people when I was younger. I've felt disappointed in myself, in my lack of ability to save everyone, and I ate my disappointment. That only led to self-loathing and feelings of unworthiness. I've used food all my life as a way to relieve loneliness, or to make myself feel better.

Now that I've figured out that flaw in myself, it's still a struggle to lose the weight that I've accumulated. I walk around wearing my imperfection for all to see, and that's heartbreaking too. Food has always been my downfall, with only two exceptions. When I'm writing or when I'm doing spirit work, something magical happens to me. Those are the only times when I actually forget to eat. At those times, I find myself absorbed in something that fills me in a different way, I guess.

Shortly after my mother died, I started learning how to do work with spirits. My desperation during that time of caregiving led me to want more connectedness, so I looked for ways to find it. I renewed my practice of Shamanic Journeying and I began training with a few teachers to actually become a spirit medium myself.

Several people over the years had advised me to pursue these studies, saying that I seemed to have a gift for being able to communicate with spirits. I have always thought that maybe I just have strongly developed intuition and empathy. Like any skill, it just takes some knowledge and a lot of practice.

The lessons and training in mediumship amazed me because I didn't quite understand how this was happening, but I started to be able to bring through impressions about spirits around me. At first, I was connecting with my own loved ones in spirit, but then I honed the skills and was able to do readings for other students. Eventually, as I learned more, I asked some friends and family members to let me practice with them, and the results astounded me.

They were able to identify the spirits coming through, and this seemed to be meaningful for them. Little by little, I realized that I was getting to be fairly good at this, and I wanted to do it more. Friends started to recommend me to other friends for spirit readings, and without much effort on my part, the work seemed to grow into a small side business for me, solely through word of mouth. I call my business *Live in the Light*, because I believe that all of this interconnectedness with our spirit friends happens within the light of love.

Similarly, people who do this type of metaphysical work are sometimes called Light Workers, meaning that the connections are being made within the light of divine. I think that's a perfect description. This work is done with a respect for the sacred that's all around us, within every ordinary thing.

None of this has been a struggle for me. It all came easily, and I have felt as if I've been doing this work, becoming a Light Worker, all of my life. The only difference is that now I'm able to give it better focus. I'm learning how to control and work with the spiritual energy around me. My best teacher has been the practice itself, as I learn new insights through the actual work.

When I started doing readings for some friends and family as a student, I was overwhelmed by the feeling. The trick is to let go of my ego and just let the spirits and their messages come through. Anyone can do this; anyone can connect with spirits around them. I believe that friends in spirit can communicate with us through the love that connects us all to one another, and I believe that every person has the capability to receive love and guidance from loved ones who have passed.

The more open we are to receiving these messages, the more clearly the messages will come through, in various ways. Friends in spirit come through to help us on our journey, to share messages and, most importantly, to bring love. Spirit readings bring healing to both the giver of the reading and the recipient. When I feel that connection to the spirit world, it makes me less fearful of dying.

When I do a reading for someone, I use all my senses (sight, sound, smell, taste and feeling) as well as extrasensory perceptions. I silently open myself to receive messages from the person's friends in spirit, and those spirits will communicate with that person through me.

Silently, like meditation, I open myself to receiving signs, impressions, feelings, and visions. As things are revealed to me, I tell the person receiving the reading what I'm experiencing. The spirit friends show me things that I understand, so that I will be prompted to say things that the person receiving the reading will understand. In other words, the spirits will get me to say what's needed for the person to identify them, even if I don't understand the reference.

For the person receiving the reading, it works almost like a puzzle. I'm given impressions, and I can present them to the recipient in pieces. Then, the recipient has to put the pieces together in a meaningful way. They just have to stay open-minded to whatever is coming through. Sometimes the messages are clear and immediately powerful, and other times the messages are more cryptic and might need further validation to completely understand them.

I have my own team of spirit friends that help me with readings and with everything I do as a Light Worker. I've done many meditations and readings to identify my team, and some of them come through for me very clearly and specifically. My father is my primary helper and he often assists me. It's almost like he's an usher, bringing other spirits through to work with me. I've found him to be steady and reliable, which is the way I like to remember him from the best times in his life, too.

Sometimes, I also call on a young friend, Andrew, who passed away a few years ago, suddenly and unexpectedly. He was primarily a close friend of Zoe, but I had met him first while I was substitute teaching and then his family joined the Quaker Meeting. He and I had a friendship of our own, and when he passed, I felt the loss deeply.

Now, I feel that I connect with him in spirit form, and he seems to be the most eager of the spirits I work with, always ready to help and to provide guidance. The way he comes through has evolved. At first, he seemed to be longing to share messages concerning his passing, especially with his family, but he soon started to bring through assurances that he was very happy and at peace on the other side. He quickly became a guardian for his family and friends.

It was almost as if he went through a training process on the other side, to learn to use his skills and talents well to help people through their earthly journeys. He actually comes through for me stronger than any other spirit friend. He sometimes wakes me up during the night with messages and impressions, and he's almost always in the room with me when I'm doing readings. I think that his youthful energy and desire to help people made him a top rate guardian and protector for those of us still living and struggling in the physical world.

As for my mother, well, she definitely comes through frequently as well. I've had some truly astonishing experiences since she passed. I've seen signs, heard song lyrics, and experienced impressions that all assure me she's around me. She started coming through for me fairly quickly after she passed. I think that she had been prepared for her transition in death, and because she firmly believed that spirits communicate with us, she was quick to be able to reconnect.

She came through clearly in a reading that I received about two months after she had passed. The medium told me that my mother was delighted that I'd reconnected with her dear friend's daughter, and that my mother was aware that her own passing was what brought us together again. That impression was absolutely correct, because my friend and I had reconciled fully at that point, and we had also spent time talking about both of our mothers and their own friendship, which had preceded ours.

My mother also came through for me strongly and directly a few months after she passed, in a way that opened me to entirely new ways to work with spirits. She actually showed herself to me, as clear as anything.

It happened one night when I couldn't sleep, and I went to sit in her former bedroom, which had become the office where I work. I sat in the armchair, which had been hers, in the corner of the room, and meditated. When I finished my meditation, I just sat for a little while and stared out the window into the dark landscape behind our house. I could see the black silhouettes of the trees with their lacy branches, but not much more than that.

I was thinking about my mother, remembering how she used to look out that same window so often, and instinctively I turned my head toward the large mirror on the wall, the mirror that had been my mother's for so many years. There, deep in the mirror, I saw my mother's face. It was as if she was standing in that dark space within the mirror, but her face was illuminated. Her expression was neutral but she was staring at me, making eye contact. I only saw her face, not her body or anything else.

It almost reminded me of the scene in the old movie *The Ghost and Mrs Muir*, when Mrs Muir looks into the dark room and sees the face of the sea captain. My mother's face had that same aura that Rex Harrison's face had in the movie, and it made me smile to think of that. My mother would know that I'd make that connection because she and I loved that movie, and we watched it together several times.

From the mirror, my mother looked at me only for a moment or two, and then her face silently faded and was gone. It didn't frighten me to see her, although it was unexpected. It assured me that she is nearby, that she is a protector for me, and that she loves me, still.

Her appearance seemed different from the other spirit encounters I'd had, because my mother showed herself within a mirror. Since that time, I've learned about scrying, which is a way to use a mirror or reflective object to try to see visual impressions of spirits or of other things in the non-physical world. I use that type of tool fairly well, and scrying allows me to see people and objects that help me bring more clarity to readings.

I also use Tarot cards, which fascinate me by their accuracy. These are simply tools for communication, and they help me to open myself to receiving whatever the spirit friends want to bring forth.

I've also learned that I can close myself to impressions when I want to, so that I don't spend all of my time receiving and interpreting messages from the non-physical world. I need to live my own life, too. But I do love knowing that these spirit friends and guides are present whenever we call on them to assist us.

I'm still learning. I still have the appetite for more knowledge, for more purpose in my life, and for more success. The negative self-image has mostly dissolved and been replaced with true, joyful self-love. I've matured, and I've found meaning in my life, and that can turn around even the ugliest and darkest thoughts. I have come to the point in my life where I try to simply feel good each day, letting myself be filled with gratitude for the gifts and privileges that have been mine in this life, while giving back and helping others as much as I can.

When that sense of true gratitude fills me, it's hard to be sad or anxious or lonely. And if I start to feel those negatives, I try to keep myself in check and look around at all the wonders of our world. Often, this isn't easy, but the secret, I think, is to remember gratitude first.

I try to remind myself to behave more like those hospice workers. I will never forget their kindness and their patience, and their willingness to serve others who are struggling. They have followed their paths to bring them to the places where they can do their important work, and they are the carriers of daily miracles. I think that it's a pretty good goal, to try to model myself after them, as much as possible.

I think about my mother more often than I thought I would. While she was living with us, I expected that I'd want to get her out of my mind someday. But it's the opposite now.

Sometimes I'll hear jingle bells ringing and my thoughts immediately go to my mother shaking her walker to summon me, or I imagine her walking toward me with those gentle bells getting louder as she approaches. It's as if she's calling out to me and I actually think that maybe she is doing just that. She's with me now in a different, more enlightened way. I believe that as souls move forward through death, they gain a broader perspective and understand things in ways that they didn't or couldn't during their earthly life.

My mother guides me now from that powerful place of love. She struggled in life to walk up the physical stairs, but metaphorically, she stepped up a little more each day until she could see the light of her heaven at the top.

I'm still climbing my own stairs. One slow step at a time, hoping to rise to my personal best and learn my life lessons along the way. My appetite for finding fulfilment continues, and that hunger seems to be what pulls me up my own stairs, but the work I'm doing now feels satisfying and hopeful. I know now that each step moving upward will eventually lead me to a new existence. My soul will continue its journey. Each step will lead me home.

My mother made it to the top of those stairs, and I know that someday she'll be waiting there for me.

My Appetite

*My appetite
is bigger than me.
And even I will admit, from under
my blanket of shame,
that that's pretty big.
Consumed
by what I consume,
the real hunger
is swallowed.
I love a good hot dog
fried to a crisp or
cooked on a grill. I cherish
the chips,
crunchy with salt. I could
rinse it all down with tears.
But I don't because
I'm numb.
I don't taste anything
except loneliness
and mediocrity.
Alone with the cheese, alone
with myself, barely
able to imagine how
I'd devour life
if I got what I really craved.
Sometimes, when the food is done,
I can smell the true flavors.
The passion, the
erotic touch of a lover,*

the dizzying journey into the
deepest kiss.
I'm starving for wild
desire, abandoning politeness
in favor of demand.
I close my eyes and
ideas buzz around me
in orgasmic bliss.
What I need, what will satisfy, is
a superlative serving.
To bite into pleasure and
fantasy, to live
honoring my need.
My appetite for life,
for joy, for
human contact,
for achievement and success,
lifts me to appreciate
my own mortality
to understand my humanity,
to forgive myself.
I want to live big,
and bigger and bigger,
so giant, I can't be contained.
Running and jumping,
I am an eight-year-old girl who
wants to tap dance
but is told that lessons are
for the girls who show off. I learn early on,
instinctively, that my family's arguments and
my father's beer are more
important
than tap shoes.
So I tap in the cellar
in plain shoes. Pretending.
But I want to show off,

dance on a stage with a spotlight.
I want to gallop on horseback,
hike to the peak of a mountain,
sing loud songs to heartfelt applause.
I want to write poetry from pain,
walk barefoot through grass,
twirling with my head thrown back,
moving easily through space,
absorbing life's energy
up through my feet
until my whole body, my
whole being, shivers with
sensation, tingles with
triumph,
feels full.

Epilogue
My Mother's Life and Legacy

She met my father in a funeral home. His best friend was the local undertaker, and my mother was close with the undertaker's wife and knew her from the Ladies' Sodality at church. My mother was the Prefect of the Sodality, of course. The undertaker couple wanted to introduce them to each other, so they invited each of my future parents to come to dinner at their home, which was part of the funeral home where they lived and worked.

My mother was twenty-seven years old, and my father was three years younger. Apparently, they saw each other and were smitten. He was the tall, handsome police officer, and she was the dainty blue-eyed blonde who was available, though most of her friends were already married. She said that she knew instantly that he was special. They dated for only one month before he proposed to her, and they weremarried less than a year later. Without question, he was the love of her life.

But my father wasn't her first love. She had been engaged once before to a man who left town with another woman just a few weeks before the wedding to my mother was supposed to take place. The invitations had already been sent out and the bridal gown was already hanging in my mother's bedroom. She was devastated.

Whenever she spoke about it to me in later years, she always sounded as though she'd dodged a bullet, admitting that it was bitterly painful at first, but that she soon realized that she was lucky he'd left. Her feelings for him changed quickly, as she recovered from that blow. But he wasn't her first love either.

She had dated a young man before that, and she had expected that she might marry him when he returned home from the war. I'm not sure how she met him, but he visited her whenever he had leave, and he asked her to wait for him. He hadn't specifically proposed, probably because he didn't know what his own future held, so she hadn't given an answer.

Sometimes, when she told the story, she would say that he was just *a very dear friend*. I think that it helped her to deal with the misery of the loss. He never returned from the war and she found out the tragic news when one of her letters was returned to her unopened, stamped *Deceased*. She talked about him every now and then, and she surprised me by bringing him up when I took her to the New Jersey shore for her eighty-ninth birthday.

It was a weekday and I'd taken a day off from work so that we could celebrate on her actual birthday. It was late September, and the weather was perfect off-season beach weather. Although, I wasn't sure if she'd need it, I packed the wheelchair that had belonged to my mother-in-law into my trunk, along with other anticipated supplies to make this adventure work well. I picked up my mother after breakfast, after she'd had time to get herself ready without rushing.

We drove the two-hour trip to Ocean City, New Jersey, and as I'd expected, she enjoyed looking at all the sites, reading signs out loud and commenting on everything we passed. We listened to Frank Sinatra and Bing Crosby as we drove, and when we got to our destination, she was overjoyed to see the ocean.

We walked just a few steps along the boardwalk before she asked for the wheelchair, which actually made things much easier. I pushed her in the chair, with a blanket over her knees, as she wore a brimmed hat, large sunglasses, and held an umbrella over her head. The beachy sunshine would not dare to penetrate her shield, because there was no visible skin.

For the record, I was wearing shorts and a tee-shirt. But it made her happy to be all covered up, and it was only mildly more difficult to push the wheelchair with the open umbrella in my face. We travelled all along the length of the boardwalk, going in and out of shops, and putting the umbrella up and down.

After one long walk down the boards and back, we stopped for lunch at an oceanfront restaurant, and she was delighted to sit by the large windows in the air conditioned place, watching people walk by outside and also watching the waves and seagulls just beyond.

After lunch, I pushed her along some more and we got ice cream cones. I was surprised because she had always wanted her ice cream in a dish for as long as I could remember, but on this day, I guess she was feeling whimsical and girlish, and she wanted to hold an ice cream cone. I parked her wheelchair under a roofed area of benches on the boardwalk, and we licked our treats and looked out at the sparkling ocean.

It was in that spot that she told me that she was thinking about her young man, and wondering whatever had happened to him, whatever he had experienced. She said that looking at the ocean reminded her of him being across the sea in military service, and she told the story to me again, no less melancholy than ever. When we finished the ice cream, we sat quietly for a while, just watching the waves and listening to the roar of the ocean, imagining its secrets.

Eventually, she broke the reverie by saying, "I guess this is the last time I'll see the ocean." I wanted to disagree, to argue that of course she'd be back here again, but I wasn't sure that she would be, and it didn't seem like a time to be anything less than honest. I think I responded to her by saying, "Maybe." It was one of the best days I ever spent with my mother. Despite all of the differences that we'd already found in each other, none of it mattered on that day. We just had a simply beautiful mother-daughter day at the shore.

For her ninetieth birthday, instead of a party, which I knew she would not want, my sisters and I involved family and friends by inviting people to send cards and letters to my house. Social media allowed me to reach out to distant relatives and friends from childhood, and I secretly took my mother's address book for a day to contact some of her old friends too. She had no idea.

I collected everything, and on the evening of her birthday, after having cake at my house with Scott, Abby and Zoe, we presented my mother with a large basket of cards and notes. Both of my sisters were on Facetime, so they could see her reactions as she read through the greetings. Some folks had sent small gifts, and two of our friends sent flowers as well. My mother was surprised and tearful and overwhelmed by the expressions of love. It was obvious that her life had touched many people.

She had always wanted to teach languages but when she put together the wording for her own obituary, she wrote that although she never had the opportunity to do that, she did teach *the language of God*. She put little stars next to this in her notes, making sure that anyone who put together her memorials would know that she considered this to be her greatest accomplishment. In fact, she wrote those very words: 'Teaching the language of God to newcomers to the Church through the RCIA program was my greatest accomplishment.'

She triple-underlined it. That was written on the page amid listings of all of her accomplishments, jobs and adventures. In the margin on that page, she wrote, 'Mother of three beautiful daughters'. At first, I was offended that motherhood was in the margin. It hurt me to see that she didn't put stars around that listing.

But I eventually realized that I needed to look at it differently, because I know that motherhood was truly her life's joy.

I know now that she didn't mean to, literally, marginalize that item on her list. She was probably super focused on listing her resume items, but then when she thought about raising her daughters, she simply couldn't leave that off the list, so she wrote it in the margin, just to be sure we would know.

Other than religion and languages, art and music were her favorite things. She painted beautiful water color landscapes and images, and she was invited to exhibit them. We used to do art projects together when I was little. One of my favorites was something that I always thought she invented, but only later learned that many people did this. She would take sheets of regular white paper and wet them in the sink, then lay them flat on wax paper.

Then we'd take my little set of watercolor paints and dip the brushes into water and then soak up a bunch of the paint and splash it onto the wet paper. It would drip and run and spread like fireworks. Sometimes, she would fold the wet painted papers in half like a card so that the wet paint would sandwich onto the other side and then the designs would be symmetrical when we opened the paper. And when the papers dried, we had our masterpieces. My childhood was really pretty good.

I also have vivid memories of my mother and eldest sister playing piano and cello duets in our living room, and those became my two favorite instruments. My mother continued to play piano at our home in Maryland until three weeks before she passed away.

My mother was also a homeroom parent for my middle sister's elementary school classes, and she let me come with her when it was her turn to serve cupcakes to my sister and her classmates. I felt so important because she let me help. My mother had a way of making each of us feel important.

Even something as simple as chopping spinach was a way to make me feel helpful and involved. *Spinach* was an activity that I loved with my mother. Whenever she'd prepare spinach for dinner, she'd give me her little wooden cutting board and a not-too-sharp knife, and she'd ask me to chop the cooked spinach.

I'd chop and chop, probably for an hour, and she'd let me do that and keep her company while she attended to the rest of the meal. But she made it seem like it was important for me to do that chopping. I did something similar when Abby was little.

Whenever I'd make her favorite macaroni and cheese from a box, I'd pour the milk into a measuring cup with the orange powdery cheese, and I'd ask Abby to stir it up for me. It was a completely unnecessary step, but it gave her a way to be involved with the preparation, and I knew that I'd learned that skill from my own mother.

I also loved it when our family would gather to look at our slides. We would have the projector and screen set up in the living room, and my mother would make snacks while my father worked the projector and dealt with his frustration at sideways and upside-down slides. We'd haul out those slides, screen and projector any time we had company, especially when there was a chance to embarrass us kids in front of our friends. But it was all done in fun.

There were hundreds of slides starting just before my eldest sister was born, and we'd watch for hours with my mother narrating what was what, but we always seemed to get tired and stop watching right around the time I was born.

My mother definitely had a fondness for anything sweet. I remember that when I'd walk with my neighborhood friends to Dairy Queen, a few blocks away, my mother always asked me to bring her a banana split or a strawberry sundae, and this was before the days of plastic lids. So, I'd carry the sundaes home with the ice cream melting down my hands.

The banana splits were bigger than the sundaes, so Dairy Queen put each banana split into a cardboard box, but it just sat loosely in the box, and as I'd walk home along the avenue, the dish inside would slide around.

By the time my mother would receive her treat, it was pretty much lining the inside of the box. But she didn't complain. She said that it still tasted the same, which was delicious.

She loved going for rides in the car, with my father smoking his Kent 100s as he drove along. She especially loved it if we could go farther outside the suburbs into the country to look for deer. The only problem was that she referred to this activity as 'deer hunting', which gave a very different impression from what we were actually doing. I remember the raised eyebrows of my friends when my mother would happily suggest, "Let's go deer hunting tonight!"

Actually, this meant that we'd be driving slowly down back roads out in the country, with my father behind the wheel, staring out the car windows on the lookout for deer that might appear in the woods. We'd stop and admire them for a few minutes from a distance and then drive on to see if we could spot any more.

She also spent hours with me on sunny afternoons, when the sunlight would come in through her bedroom windows, holding her rainbow maker to the light. We'd sit together in her rocking chair, me on her lap or leaning on the windowsill, and we'd take turns trying to catch beams of light onto the small Lucite prism that her father had made for her when she was young. He'd meant it to be a pendant and he made it from a small leftover piece of Lucite when he was working as a tool and die maker at the RCA Company in New Jersey.

He'd made her the small pendant to wear like jewelry, but she soon realized that it could catch the light and cast tiny rainbows if she held it up. And we did that together so often on those afternoons in my parents' bedroom, making rainbows of light on the dark blue rug.

When she lived with us in Maryland, I brought out the rainbow maker one afternoon, because she had given it to me several years earlier, and I was heartbroken when she didn't recognize what it was or what it did. I had to show her how it worked and I had to remind her that Opa had made it for her. She enjoyed it but she just didn't remember it.

It was one of the sure signs to me that she was declining, because that little trinket had been so special to her. The rainbow maker was one of my favorite memories of time spent with my mother as I was growing up.

But her life didn't begin when she became a mother. There was so much more to her story. She was born in 1925 to German immigrant parents, but her father, my Opa, had dual citizenship in Germany and the U.S.A., so her parents had arrived in America as citizens. They didn't speak English and my mother spoke only German until she started school.

Gradually, she taught English to her parents, which was the beginning of her love for languages. She later learned to speak French as well, and she often told the funny story of being chosen as the president of the Spanish Club at her high school, even though she barely spoke Spanish. Apparently, the teachers knew that she'd try to learn. She always wanted to know more about everything. She especially loved stories of history and geography.

My mother graduated from Philadelphia High School for Girls, and she spoke fondly of her graduation ceremony with all of the graduating girls wearing floor length white gowns and carrying bouquets of American Beauty red roses. The famous contralto Marian Anderson, who was known for performing operas and spirituals, as well as for overcoming racial prejudice, was present at my mother's high school graduation.

Marian Anderson's niece was one of my mother's classmates, and my mother felt a thrill at seeing one of her favorite musicians seated there in the audience. My mother said that as she walked up the aisle at the conclusion of the graduation, she spotted Ms. Anderson and felt herself staring in awe, and Marian Anderson smiled at her. My mother never forgot that.

Even when my mother was living with us, she told the hospice chaplain about Marian Anderson at the graduation, and I was able to find some recordings of her performances on YouTube and played them for my mother on my phone. The look on my mother's face was pure joy.

My mother sang with several prestigious singing societies, and she also sang and performed with my grandparents in German-language radio shows. She worked occasionally as an accompanist, playing piano brilliantly, and in my opinion, one of her greatest engagements as a pianist was being the temporary accompanist for my elementary school choir. I felt so proud to have her sitting there at the piano next to our choir director as my friends and I stood on the bleachers singing!

She also graduated from Taylor School of Business and worked as a Legal Secretary, often serving as an interpreter in court cases involving German speaking witnesses and claimants. My mother was invited by one of the partners in the law firm where she worked to accompany him to participate in the Nuremberg trials, but she declined. She felt that she would not have been able to handle the horrific evidence that would have been presented.

My mother often told a story that she had been told by her own mother, my Oma. Oma grew up in Germany, one of twelve children plus three more step-children, in a very poor family. Oma carried her lunch with her to school, and she always had dry bread, sometimes with a little bit of homemade butter or jam. There was a girl at Oma's school whose father was a merchant and had a shop in their town.

That girl brought meats and fruit with her lunch, but she extended an unbelievable amount of kindness to her poor classmate. Oma remembered that almost every day, this young girl would beg her to trade lunches. She would tell Oma that she preferred Oma's fresh baked bread to the things her parents gave her, and so Oma, being a young girl and not seeing through the gesture, gladly traded for the more nutritious food.

When Oma, and then my mother, would tell this story, they'd say that the girl was like an angel, one of the kindest people ever, and that she was obviously taught well by her family, taught to be kind and caring without showing pity. That girl and her family were Jewish, and Oma would often tearfully say that she would never know what happened to her as a German Jew. She imagined that the girl and her family were gone.

My mother never let me forget that story growing up, and she told it with the same tenderness as if it had been her own story. She used it to illustrate the utter unfairness and brutality of prejudices, and the despicable acts that humans are capable of.

I think that my recollection of that story, and of my mother's desire to treat all people fairly, made me especially disappointed when my mother initially objected to me marrying a Jewish man. She clearly changed her opinion about Scott over the years, even choosing him to be my back-up as her healthcare proxy and executor of her will, because she trusted him completely, but it wasn't like that at first. Our painful engagement discussion was proof of that. When she first realized that he and I were serious about each other, she wasn't pleased.

Even after we were married, there were signs of her displeasure. On some Jewish holidays like Hanukkah and Passover, which we celebrated with our daughters, my mother would call and tell me to wish Scott a happy holiday, not including me or the girls in the wish. She couldn't bear the thought that we were possibly letting go of my Christianity.

She and my father did warm up eventually, and they often came to our house for Jewish celebrations and holidays, along with my in-laws, and we had some wonderful times together. We celebrated everything, and both sides of our extended family participated in all the holidays, and they eventually came to love each other. But I always felt the slight disapproval of my choices just below the surface of the pleasantry with my parents.

It was fine for Scott to celebrate his heritage, but it wasn't fine for me to do it too. They simply wanted me to be Catholic. Yet, my parents took part in our Seder meals and the lighting of the menorah, and they especially enjoyed many potato latkes at our house. They also treated Scott's brother's daughters, who were being raised Jewish, with love and affection, almost as if they were her granddaughters too. So, I believe that they were trying their best.

My mother had some struggles to overcome as well. She stopped driving when she was in her early fifties. She had been involved in two car accidents that left her too nervous to drive again. One was minor and no one was hurt, but the other was a major incident in which my mother's 1966 Plymouth Fury was hit from behind while she was stopped at a red light, causing her car to lunge forward and strike a blind pedestrian who was crossing in front of her car.

Neither crash was her fault but both contributed to her lifelong anxiety, not only about driving, but about anything that happened unexpectedly or without her control.

As a young child, my mother had polio, and throughout her life, she suffered from Post-Polio Syndrome, which she only found a name for in the later years of her life. The syndrome, which is a disorder of the muscles and nerves, caused her to feel exhausted fairly often. It involved muscle weakness that worsens over time, and she was often in pain, especially in her joints.

Her left leg was slightly thinner than her right leg, but she was very grateful that she was able to walk at all. She credited her father, who had tightened the pedals on her tricycle so that she had to really use her leg muscles to ride. I believe that after his own soccer injury years earlier, when he'd been told that he'd never walk again, he wasn't going to stand by without attempting to find ways to help his daughter heal her legs.

She said that he walked all around the neighborhood with her as she rode along on that special tricycle, and he'd walk for hours, forcing her to exercise her legs. His efforts worked, and she walked and danced throughout her life.

I have gorgeous photos of my mother when she was a young woman and had been working in a local bank. She and some other female employees, including her dearest friend, my Aunt Loretta, were chosen to pose at the historic Valley Green Inn in Philadelphia. To me, my mother looked like a fashion model, and as I grew up looking at those photos and other photos too, I could hardly imagine that she'd ever suffered physically. She seemed perfect to me.

Part of her perfection was in her clothing. She had given me a hamper filled with her discarded clothing that I used when I frequently played dress-up. I'd play by myself and sometimes with friends in our basement, and I loved putting on her dresses and shoes, right over my own clothes and socks. I'd twirl around and pretend to be a princess and her clothes were perfect for that.

I can still see my two favorite dresses so clearly in my memory. One was a white cotton sleeveless dress with tiny bright red polka dots all over it, and it had a flowy skirt with a ruffle at the bottom. It was beautiful and soft, and I wore it all the time. The other was a blue satin dress with an A-line skirt and a stylish flat bow on the front.

That was my alternate, and I'd switch between those two dresses most often, despite all the other clothes in the hamper. Both dresses dragged on the floor when I wore them at play, but they were probably just below the knee when my mother had worn them for real. As I think about those dresses now, I realize that they were absolutely gorgeous garments, and my mother must have been beautiful in them. It gives me the impression of her being a princess, like Grace Kelly, who was actually my mother's favorite actress.

By far, the highlight of my mother's life was being married to my father. First and foremost, she was his dutiful and beautiful wife, and for the most part, they made each other happy. I think that she took her identity from him, and her role was to be the homemaker and to have dinner ready when he got home from work.

I remember that my father would usually come in the door, put down his briefcase and wash his hands, and then sit right down at the table to eat. She'd start putting our evening meal into the serving bowls and platters as soon as she saw him pulling into the driveway behind our rowhome.

They went to formal events for the Knights of Columbus and the Ladies' Sodality, both at our parish, and we have photos of them as a strikingly handsome couple. Their involvement at church was always important to them, and I remember well my father's wrath if any of his daughters showed up at church late for Sunday mass or dressed too casually. In their later years, they worked together in the RCIA program, initiating newcomers to the Catholic faith.

They made many friends through that program, and there were many younger adults who would say that my parents had been like parents to them. I'm sure that my parents were delighted to be bringing so many new Catholics into the parish, and I'm also sure that my departure from Catholicism was embarrassing for them.

In their retirement years, my parents took trips together to Ireland and continental Europe. They also drove all over Pennsylvania, and they probably knew every road through the Pocono Mountains. One summer, years earlier, my parents and I drove across the U.S.A. from Pennsylvania to Texas to visit my eldest sister who was living there, and I sat in the backseat of my father's car all through the Smokey Mountains and southern states on the way there, and through more northern states on the way back.

The three of us stopped in Nashville, Memphis, and at any scenic spot we could find, staying in motels that we'd find along the way. I remember a lot of laughter on that trip but we didn't have to fuss over the radio, because I'd made mix tapes to play in the cassette player, enough for the whole ride. I had the tapes in a shoebox, and I included music that my parents enjoyed, even Swing music and Irish folk songs, as well as pop songs for myself.

Nothing too mellow, so that my father wouldn't get drowsy behind the wheel. My mother acted as DJ, since I was in the back seat, and she'd select a new tape each time one finished. She said that she really enjoyed the mix of music, and my father said that it wasn't too bad either.

Because I knew that my parents loved going for drives so much, it was difficult for me to argue with them as I became an adult, when they'd so often pop in to see me—at college, at my apartment, at places that I'd tell them I was going—under the premise of saying, "*We happened to be driving by.*" There were a few near-misses in college when they'd show up on a weekend morning just as we were cleaning up from a party the night before. I knew that they were checking up on me.

It was the same with my apartments. They'd show up unannounced and knock on the door, expecting me to be available to spend time with them. Once, when I finally had an apartment on my own without a roommate, I'd asked my father to sit in my apartment while a plumber was working in my kitchen, because I needed to be at work. My father was not working at the time, so his day was free.

I'd left a key with him, and when the plumber had finished, my father took my key to the hardware store down the street and had a copy made for himself. He told me that he was going to keep it for emergencies. He didn't ask me; he told me. I'm sure that he could see my trepidation, and it proved to be a reasonable fear, because my parents indeed went to my apartment several times when I wasn't home, always without prior arrangements, to drop off something my mother had baked or to bring me a piece of mail that went to their house. They'd go into my apartment while I was at work.

Twice, I woke up on weekends to find that my parents had been in my apartment while I was asleep in my bedroom. I was in my late twenties at that time and they saw no problem with letting themselves into my apartment. I tried repeatedly to convince them not to do it again, and I even asked for the key back, but they insinuated that I was up to something suspicious if it wasn't okay for them to come into my apartment.

I'm sure that they were checking to see if I was alone, to see if Scott's car was at my apartment, and also to make sure that I wasn't waking up somewhere else. If any of those things had happened when my parents stopped in unexpectedly, then they'd accuse me of ruining their good name. Thankfully, they never caught me in anything that they would have deemed inappropriate. When Scott and I got married, I didn't give them a key to our house.

We gave them a key later, when Abby was a year and a half old, and I was pregnant with Zoe. My first pregnancy wasn't easy because I had edema, but my second was really rough. It was so dangerous that my doctors told me not to try to have more children after that. I started having gall bladder attacks shortly into that pregnancy and I wound up having my gall bladder removed in a major surgery, with a ten inch incision, when I was seven months pregnant.

I'd been hospitalized after a particularly bad attack, and on the morning of Memorial Day, the doctor came to my room and looked at my bloodwork results, and then they rushed me into surgery immediately. I later learned that I had pancreatitis with my Amylase protein at a life-threatening level. I woke up from the surgery still intubated, with a row of staples across my belly, wondering whether or not I was still pregnant. I was, thankfully.

The surgeon told me, with a little laugh, that he'd 'met the baby' and all looked good. I am forever grateful for the miracle of his skill in operating on my pregnant-self successfully. But I had to go onto bedrest at home for the remainder of my pregnancy and I already had a toddler at home.

Without hesitation, my parents agreed to come to our house every day to be with Abby while I rested on the sofa or in my bed. They'd arrive before Scott left for work, so that my mother would be on hand to lift Abby out of her crib or into her high chair. Sometimes, my father would drop off my mother, and then he'd go to do their errands or he'd go back home if he was tired that day. But many days they both stayed.

They'd play with Abby and entertain her all day, and occasionally Abby would run over to me for a hug. It broke my heart that I couldn't pick her up, so I hugged her as much as I could while lying down. Sometimes, the pain from my surgical incision and staples was too severe, and I'd have to go to my bedroom, and that made me sad too.

I wanted to be with Abby every moment, especially because I knew my attention would be divided when the new baby arrived. But Abby was in capable hands. My parents fed her and put her down for naps, and although, our parenting styles were different, they tried to follow our instructions with Abby.

I'll admit that I wasn't always happy about having my parents in my house every day, but I had to get over that and appreciate that they were helping me in an enormous way. But they commented on everything, judged everything they noticed, and my mother frequently had the pursed lips and unmoving expression that told me something was wrong, that she'd observed something she didn't like.

I was also bothered by my mother constantly telling Abby that it was her job to take care of me and make me feel better. Abby was a very precocious toddler and she could talk and seemed very capable of things beyond her years. But I'd learned that it's not always a good idea to tell little children that they are responsible for things that they can't control, and I talked with my mother about that several times.

I asked her to be careful about the way she phrased things, and to please stop telling Abby, who wasn't even two years old yet, that it was her job to take care of me. If something went wrong with me, I didn't want Abby to feel any guilt, and I didn't think I was out of the woods yet. I was already worried that Abby might be having some anxiousness about me not being able to play with her. She knew that things had changed.

I had no problem with teaching Abby to assist me and encouraging her to be kind and helpful, even to ask me if I needed anything. But I wanted my mother to stop making it seem like it was Abby's responsibility, which she did almost daily, complete with a humorous finger wag at Abby's face, as she'd say, "It's your job to take care of your Mommy and help her get better." I remember the very serious look on Abby's little face, as if she was internalizing this warning.

I remembered feeling that way myself, like I had the responsibility of healing my family when I was young, and I didn't want that for Abby. But when I'd try to talk with her, my mother basically told me that I was being ridiculous and continued to tell Abby that she had to be my nurse and to 'make sure' I was comfortable, which might have been okay if it was made into a game.

It just didn't sound as playful as my mother may have intended it. Most upsetting to me, she continued to say to Abby, 'this is your job'. I knew that Abby wouldn't remember the words, but I worried that she might be imprinting the feeling and the pressure, especially from this impressionable age. She was still a baby herself. It just wasn't what I wanted her to be hearing when everything was already so mixed up at our house.

But in fairness, my mother's gifts to Abby far outnumbered my concerns. She spent countless hours drawing crayon pictures with Abby, playing with her dolls and toys and reading to her so gently, and I think that Abby inherited some of my mother's quiet and calm personality. My parents were life savers for our family. They had also stayed with Abby while I was in the hospital, so I was able to rest and recover.

When I first got home from the hospital after my surgery, after I'd been away from Abby for several days, she was asleep for a nap when I came in the door. But she must have heard us coming in and talking to my parents, and she started to call out to me. From my doctor's instructions, I was supposed to lie down right away but I went into Abby's room with my mother and knelt down next to Abby's little toddler bed.

I kissed and hugged her because I couldn't lift her up, so we just stayed there with me on my knees for a little while. My mother told me later that she wouldn't ever forget that image of me and Abby hugging each other, so happy to be together again. She actually said that it was the most beautiful thing she'd ever seen, and she told me that I was a good mother. I treasured those words. I still do.

She was a very good mother too. I believe that she did the very best that she could, and it was honestly pretty wonderful. She was, almost always, very kind.

Eventually, though, my mother became the old woman of the family. She became the stereotypical grandmother, with quirks and peculiarities that we all laughed about. She told everyone she met in Maryland that, because she was now living in horse country, she was going to start training to become the first ninety-four-year-old jockey to ride in the Preakness Stakes horse race.

She joked that she was going to give herself a year for the training, and that she'd enter the race after her ninety-fourth birthday. She didn't know that she wouldn't see that age, that she wouldn't make it past ninety-three.

She became a woman who sat with Scott watching the Philadelphia Sixers play basketball on TV, cheering when he cheered, groaning when he groaned, and then asking him questions like, "Which ones are the Sixers?" even though the game was almost over. She enjoyed Scott's company. They also watched bowling together. Scott wasn't especially a fan, but for some unexplainable reason, my mother thought that watching bowling on TV was hilarious, and Scott laughed with her, as hard as she did.

She was extremely proud of her five grandchildren and she spoke about them often and bragged about them to anyone who would listen. Her first great grandchild was born just a month before my mother passed, and she was thrilled about the beautiful baby girl. Without realizing that it was a family name, my nephew and his wife named their baby girl with a variation of my Oma's first name.

My mother knew that it wasn't deliberate because the young parents weren't aiming for a family name, but she felt that God had a hand in that. I'll admit that I felt the same way.

I printed some photos of the new baby and made my mother a little photo album. She proudly showed it to all the hospice workers and took it with her when she went to respite care. She used to sit in the den, just paging through the photos of her new great-granddaughter, smiling and crying as she looked at each picture. She wished that she could meet her in person, but that didn't happen either.

We filmed a little video of my mother holding the photo album and talking about how happy she was to have the new baby in our family, and I sent it to my nephew in hopes that his sweet little girl would someday be able to watch it and know that her great-grandmother loved her so much. All of the grandchildren would receive photo albums that my mother had compiled herself, but her great-granddaughter came along after my mother was no longer able to do that kind of project. Talking on the little video was all she could manage.

My mother also made albums for my sisters and me. Mine sat on her bookshelf in our den while she lived with us, as she had put the albums together long before we moved. Each album had our baby photos—well, the ones that were actual prints, instead of being part of our slides—and followed our growth through awkward adolescence. After she died, I pulled my album down off the shelf to look through it more carefully, and I noticed that she had tucked some newspaper clippings into the front of the book.

The clippings were articles that had been published in Philadelphia newspapers about work that I had helped to do on Benjamin Lay, a historic Quaker abolitionist who had been a member of Abington Friends Meeting, where I worked and worshiped. Benjamin Lay had been known for dramatic stunts to call attention to the urgent need to abolish slavery immediately, but his story had been somewhat forgotten over the years. I was one of the team that helped to bring some recognition to his legacy.

My mother had saved the clippings in my photo album. She must have been proud of that work that I'd done, and those clippings showed me that maybe she wasn't too disappointed in me after all.

Despite what my mother said about her greatest accomplishment being the RCIA program, I have my own opinion about the way that she *really* spoke God's language. When I think of what defined my mother's life for me, I come away with two things that seem most important. I remember her tucking me in and kissing me goodnight at bedtime, making me feel safe and loved every night, and I remember how she took care of Oma and Opa so gracefully when they lived with us and needed her constant care to manage each day's activities. I feel glad that I was able to do some of those things for her at the end of her life.

My mother and I had a relationship that was like the old Vaudeville joke: *"What would you ever do without me?...I don't know, but I'd sure like to find out!"* But we also knew that it was only a joke. We needed each other more than either of us realized.

My mother was a very private person. As she sat with me all those times planning her own funeral, she often mentioned that she didn't want anything posted on social media about her funeral arrangements. She gave me permission to post a memorial that would only be seen by friends of those tagged, and those tagged would only be family.

And yet, she was a person who vehemently wanted to be remembered. She asked me countless times to make sure to tell stories about her to her grandchildren and great-grandchildren, just as she had frequently told stories to me and to my sisters about our grandparents, going back several generations.

This was a woman who spent countless hours, with no computer, compiling a family history, including a small booklet with photos, so that all of her descendants could have the information. Legacy was important to her and she made that abundantly clear.

But would she have liked the stories I've shared in this book? I hope so. There are many stories that I've omitted for her privacy, and because I don't want to be disrespectful of my dear mother. The glimpses I've chosen to share are the ones that best illustrate our struggle together and the healing that happened between us.

During her life, my mother labelled me as *The Writer* in our family. Whether or not I deserved that title, she continually encouraged me to write and to try to get published more. "Just keep writing," she'd say.

She often told me, from the time I was in elementary school, that she thought that my writing could help people. With that in mind, I embarked on this writing adventure, trusting that I'd be able to capture her story and mine in a way that she'd approve of. That being said, I hesitated quite a lot while writing this book to question myself and to second-guess the way forward.

During the course of this writing project, I received several spirit readings in which I was encouraged to keep writing. *Keep working on the book*, my loved ones in spirit advised. I heard this same refrain in almost every reading, including Tarot readings, provided to me by a variety of people. Most importantly, I heard this message from my mother several times. *It's important; keep writing. Tell our story.*

I feel as though my mother has not only given me permission to share about our life together, but she has actually encouraged me, both before and after she passed over.

I did my best for her. I am flawed and so was she. But in the end, we belonged to each other. On her last day in this life, in her closing moment when she was taking her final few breaths before her transition into death, I believe that she knew that I was there. I was with her at the end, and always. And despite all of our differences, what remains is love.

I will always be grateful to my mother for everything she gave me in life: For her example of kindness, patience, and unconditional love. For her gift of the spoken word and storytelling, and for providing me the education needed to write down my own stories. For her humor, for her cheerfulness, and for giving me life itself.

And mostly, I'm grateful for our mutual forgiving.

Sleep tight, my good friend.

My Mother's Life

Like a bluebird resting on a flowering branch
or Snow White singing in the cottage in the woods,
she moved through Life with the grace of
a storybook princess
who wanted more, but she had a secret.
She was content.
She was happy
with all that God gave her
which was plenty, really.
Her hands held mine when I cried, and
when I needed her guidance, or
when I just wanted to look at
her hand holding mine. With the half moons
on each perfect fingernail,
she offered strength,
more than we knew,
more than we appreciated.
She spoke like a song, like
lyrics already written
on lovely melodic lines
soothing us all with her laughter.
And her best accomplishment, she said,
was speaking God's language—
not us, not me.
But maybe I would have been her legacy
if I hadn't disappointed her
as we disappointed each other.
But truly, I know.
I know that it was me and us all along.

*I know that her greatest
achievement, her
most enormous
bequest was leaving us all
her love.*

Acknowledgments

I am grateful for the time I had with my mother, the years of growing together and learning about one another, because that mother-daughter connection gave me my foundation, and it also gave me my story. My relationship with my mother was my own. I know that my family members, especially my two older sisters, probably saw her differently. Even my husband and daughters, who also lived close to my mother and wound up in the same house with my mother, had relationships with her that were unique to them. This story is simply my own, showing my mother as only I experienced her.

This book would not have been possible without the support and assistance of many people.

My heartfelt thanks go to my family members and friends who were early readers for me, and who encouraged me along this journey of sharing my story.

To my sisters, thank you for the support while I was caring for our mother.

To my spiritual teachers and guides, and there have been many, you have my eternal gratitude for lifting me up and opening my eyes.

To the Friends at Abington Monthly Meeting, thank you for teaching me to appreciate the Light within every person, for giving me a name for Continuing Revelation, and for supporting me while I was caring for my dying mother and as I struggled through bereavement.

Grateful thanks to Stella Maris Hospice in Maryland for the beautiful care they gave to my mother and to my family. Thanks especially to Sonia for the help and support, and also to Matisha, Ashley, Kelly, Fidelia and the entire hospice staff. You are heroes.

To Abington Choral Club in Pennsylvania, thank you for giving me the gift of songs and lyrics that continue to sing through my memory.

For *Purlie*, a musical with a book by Ossie Davis, Philip Rose, and Peter Udell, lyrics by Udell and music by Gary Geld. Thank you for your inspirational song, 'Walk Him Up the Stairs', which added to my appreciation of our literal and figurative walks on those stairs.

To Austin Macauley Publishers, you have my gratitude for working with me to bring this story to readers.

Most importantly, my deep and profound thanks go to my husband, Scott, my daughters, Abby and Zoe, and my son-in-law, Alan, for being with me on this journey.

And my eternal full-hearted thanks to my mother, my father, my grandparents, Friend Andrew, and my support team of loved ones in spirit for being with me and guiding my path.

Made in the USA
Middletown, DE
06 March 2024

50920323R00115